ECONOMICS OF CORRUPTION

RECENT ECONOMIC THOUGHT SERIES

Editors:

Warren J. Samuels
Michigan State University
East Lansing, Michigan, USA

William Darity, Jr.
University of North Carolina
Chapel Hill, North Carolina, USA

Other books in the series:

ECONOMICS OF CORRUPTION

Edited by

Arvind K. Jain
Concordia University

KLUWER ACADEMIC PUBLISHERS
BOSTON / DORDRECHT / LONDON

Distributors for North, Central and South America:
Kluwer Academic Publishers
101 Philip Drive
Assinippi Park
Norwell, Massachusetts 02061 USA
Telephone (781) 871-6600
Fax (781) 871-6528
E-Mail <kluwer@wkap.com>

Distributors for all other countries:
Kluwer Academic Publishers Group
Distribution Centre
Post Office Box 322
3300 AH Dordrecht, THE NETHERLANDS
Telephone 31 78 6392 392
Fax 31 78 6546 474
E-Mail <orderdept@wkap.nl>

 Electronic Services <http://www.wkap.nl>

Library of Congress Cataloging-in-Publication Data

Jain, Arvind K., 1945–
    Economics of corruption / edited by Arvind K. Jain.
        p.   cm.   — (Recent economic thought series ; 65)
    Includes bibliographical references and index.
    ISBN 0-7923-8333-8
    1. Political corruption—Economic aspects. 2. Corruption—Economic
aspects.   I. Title. II. Series.
JF1081.J34   1998
330.9—dc21   98-42253
                                                    CIP

Printed on acid-free paper.

Printed in the United States of America.

Contents

PREFACE

Corruption is nothing new. Daniel Kaufmann, one of the contributors to this volume, likes to quote from an ancient Indian manuscript almost 2500 years old. This manuscript, *The Arthshastra*, perhaps one of the oldest treatise on economics, recognizes the impact of corruption on the conduct of the economy and urges king's administrators to identify and combat corruption. In this sense, perhaps ancient economists knew something that most modern ones do not. The industry for the study of corruption went into a long decline after Kautilya. Modern economics, with the exception of the past about five years, has paid scant attention to how corruption might affect performance of economies and hence to what may cause it or how it could be measured. This is not to imply that no one raised the issue; academic as well as practitioners' voices in diverse fields such as economics, politics, government, and sociology could he heard – but only if one paid attention. Fortunately, there now appears to have been a sea change in the attitude of the economists towards corruption. The number of articles and books being devoted to this subject has grown exponentially in the 1990s. Although the change in the attitude may have commenced some time ago, it was greatly aided by the announcement of the president of the World Bank, Mr. James Wolfensohn, at the annual meeting of the Bank in 1996. He announced that the two big international institutions, the World Bank and the IMF, would treat elimination of corruption as one of the central planks of their development efforts.

This volume has grown out of the editor's study of the 1982-debt crisis. While the mainstream economists were busy dissecting economic policy errors, a small group of observers, mostly on the fringe of the international-financial-institutions-network, were urging anyone who would listen to pay attention to the behavior of the decision makers. They could see that loans that precipitated the crisis were not always made on the basis of economic efficiency. They could also sense that economic policies of the government often had the objective of hiding the consequences of what were bad loans to begin with. As could have been expected from the economic profession, however, these views were ignored almost completely not only by the borrowing countries' government but also by the lending countries' governments and by the international financial institutions. As Mr. Wolfenshon has admitted, "We didn't get everything right in the past." My own work on the debt crisis had led me to believe that a study of the debt crisis had to include an examination of the decision making process, not only of the economic decisions.

This volume owes its existence to Sandy Darity. It was his foresight and confidence that led him to invite me to edit a volume related to corruption for Kluwer Academic's series on Recent Economic Thoughts. He had been aware of my interest and work in trying to explain politicians' and bureaucrats' behavior for a long time, but it would never have occurred to me to invite a group of experts far more knowledgeable about corruption than myself to write for a joint volume. I owe Sandy gratitude and many thanks.

Other people have helped in different ways to improve the contents of this volume. Katrin Kopvillem read earlier drafts of many chapters and made important editorial suggestions. The editorial staff at Kluwer, Ranak Jasani, Yana Lambert, and Suzzane St. Clair, provided expert help at various stages. I am indebted to all of them for their help.

Arvind K. Jain
Concordia University
Montreal
Canada

1

CORRUPTION: AN INTRODUCTION

ARVIND K. JAIN
Concordia University

Corruption has been part of our economic and political life since ancient times. Stories of corruption in most advanced to most underdeveloped economies abound. In the recent years, Italy and Japan were often in headlines with stories of corruption scandals involving top level politicians. In Canada, Cameron's expose of misuse of power by a former prime minister seemed to have shocked no one, although his party was reduced to 2 seats, after having held the majority, in the parliament in the general elections following his departure (Cameron 1994). In the developing world, no one seems to be surprised by stories of corruption in countries like Haiti and Zaire; corruption now threatens to destabilize even relatively advanced democracies like India (Stackhouse 1994) and countries like China that have had a stable political system.

There is some evidence that the extent of corruption has increased during the past decade.[1] It takes many forms, most common of which are bribery of public officials, improper use and waste of public funds, or, misuse of political power to appropriate economic benefits by those in positions of power. Its prevalence and potential consequences, however, seem to far exceed the attention this phenomenon has received from economists, political scientists, or sociologists.[2]

Traditionally, macro economic theory takes only a superficial account of corruption in developing economic policy.[3] Even under the umbrella of rent seeking, the issue of corruption does not merit a subsection in the classification of Journal of Economic Literature. Evidence that corruption may influence policy making is ignored.[4] Assessments of economic performance, and even crisis, rarely examine if corruption may have contributed in any significant way to a crisis.[5]

A striking example of how we handle corruption at the highest levels in the government is provided by the third world "debt bomb" of 1980s. In August 1982, Mexico shook the foundations of the global economy when it declared that it could not make payments on its international debts. Developments during the subsequent months were to raise questions about the stability and even the continuity of the international financial system. About a year after the Mexican announcement, a joint committee of US congress sponsored a workshop to understand why the crisis had come about and how the US government should respond to it. By that time the fire fighting had been done and it would have been time to take stock. The experts who participated in this workshop presented detailed analyses of Mexican economic and political situation, but not one mention was made of the possibility that corruption may have had something to do with the financial problems of the country (Committee of Foreign Affairs 1984). In a recent analysis of the lost decade in Latin America, Dornbusch and Edwards, trying to explain this region's "proclivity toward macroeconomic mismanagement," find the answer in certain "<u>macroeconomic</u> policies" (1991: 1). Evidence of corruption was everywhere if one wanted to see. The head of PEMEX, the Mexico's government owned petroleum company that had been the recipient of the largest share of foreign funds borrowed by the Mexican government had been accused of involvement in frauds for amounts that reached a billion dollars and Mexican president Lopez Portillo was widely known to have followed policies that enriched him and his associates at the expense of the Mexican economy. Crisis was to continue till the end of the decade with serious consequences for Mexicans (Jain 1993); the international system, fortunately, rode the crisis out and ended the decade in good health.

Most of the discussion of corruption, with some exceptions in the last few years, has been considered marginal to the mainstream economic theory. This benign neglect is not justified by observable consequences of corrupt activities of those who design or implement economic policies. In some cases, admittedly the extreme ones, corrupt leaders have been able to distort economic policies to channel large proportions of their countries' resources to their own benefit at the cost of the rest of the population (Jain 1993, Naylor 1987). Economic policy becomes the tool by which the corrupt leaders redistribute national income in their favor. In these cases, corruption affects the total income that a society is able to generate, as well as the distribution of income between the leaders and the populace.[6]

In this extreme form, corruption can completely undermine the economic welfare and growth of a country. An excellent study for such a situation has been done by Klitgaard (1990). The most commonly cited examples are well known: Zaire under Mobutu regime - estimates of whose wealth reached $ 9 billion in 1997 and who was known to hire a concord to travel from his capital to France for appointments with his dentist (newspaper accounts in September 1997), Philippines under Marcos till 1985, Nicaragua under Somoza in the 1960s and 1970s, etc.

In other, simpler, forms corruption enriches owners of some resources and corrupt government officials at the cost of honest resource owners. In the United States, sugar quotas are an example of this type of corruption. A 1988 Commerce Department study concluded that contributions by sugar lobby helped keep sugar quotas and price support programs which cost American consumers about $3 billion a year. The study concluded that "Of the 29 senators who received $15,000 or more from the sugar industry, 85% voted to keep the price support program, while senators who received no contributions from the industry all voted against the subsidy." (Wall Street Journal 1991: A7). In Canada, Cameron (1994) has published an exposé of corruption in Mulroney's administration. Within these extreme forms, corruption leads to economic stagnation.[7]

The apparent neglect of the study of this phenomenon in economics may be explained by at least two area of disagreement. First, there is no agreement on what corruption really means, and second, it is difficult to model effects of corruption on economic performance.

The disagreement on what corruption means may arise because the term corruption is used to include a wide range of activities. These activities range from simple misuse of bureaucratic power by government officials to redirection of a country's wealth for the benefit of those in positions of power. The simplest case of bureaucratic corruption involves a bribe which speeds up processing of administrative procedures. Even this simple type of corruption can occur in at least two varieties. A bribe may sometimes be accompanied by an implicit (or even explicit) promise that the payment of a bribe guarantees performance - in which case the bribe-giver can view the bribe as a tax. In other cases, a bribe assures nothing. There may be future demands for bribe from the same official or from others, or the official may merely promise to look into the situation for a price. The bribe-giver, in this case, may be merely increasing his chances of success by giving bribe. A variation of the first kind of bribe is known to exist in India: officials inform potential users of the bureaucracy that they cannot guarantee performance but a bribe will ensure that the competitor will not be allowed to complete the procedures. More complex cases of bureaucratic corruption involve nepotism or influencing the design of legislation. One of the most succinct definitions of corruption[8], "... sale by government officials of government property for personal gains" covers cases in which a corrupt bureaucrat appropriates rents that legitimately belongs to the government by exercising power to speed up or delay processing of information as well as the complex case of influencing government policy or legislation that would establish property rights for owners of certain resources and hence increase the rent associated with those resources. Economists seem not to have yet developed a vocabulary, leave alone a theory, that can explain the wide range of activities that come under the umbrella of corruption.

The second problem with incorporating corruption into economic policy stems from a difficulty in establishing how corruption influences policy making and economic performance. Although the consequences of "rent seeking" or "directly unproductive activities (or DUP)" have been identified and documented, corruption involves more than rent seeking or DUP activities and its influence is difficult to model and measure.[9] It is only recently that economists have begun to make some inroads in this area.

From the perspective of theories of public choice, there is an additional problem of explaining how corruption can exist when it reduces wealth of at least some economic entities. Existence of corruption would appear to be at odds with working of free markets. Why would entities that lose due to corruption not be able to exert their influence such that corruption is eliminated? One could even ask why the losing entities would not "buy" the corruption out of the system.[10] In the absence of formal models that explain economics and politics of corruption, it is difficult to identify where the market failures take place.

During the past few years, however, there has been a resurgence of interest in understanding impact that corruption has had on our societies.[11] A major impetus for this interest has come from the concern of international organizations about the importance of governance.[12] It has become clear that development efforts will have little impact unless the recipient countries have political and economic institutions in place that allow the populace to develop and exploit its potential. The collapse of previously centrally-planned economies has also raised important questions about the importance of governance. Corruption - defined very broadly - seems to play a central role in the performance of the political apparatus regardless of the nature of the economic system - market based or socialist.

This book has two aims. First, it attempts to bring together essential elements of various approaches that have been used to understand corruption. This attempt is justified on the belief that the effects of corruption are often far more serious than is generally recognized. Recent studies and analyses of corruption point to influence of corruption reaching far beyond the people directly involved in such activities (Murphy, Shleifer and Vishny, 1991, 1993, Shleifer and Vishny, 1993, Tanzi 1995, Muaro 1995 and 1997, Elliot 1997, Kaufmann 1997, Tanzi and Davoodi 1997, Johnson, Kaufmann and Zoido-Lobaton 1998). Second, some of the contributions in this volume will attempt to shift the focus of studies on corruption away from bribery type of activities to corruption that results in distortion of economic policies. The former type of corruption has been easier to study since it is easily observed, recognized and identified. The more insidious type of corruption - the type which causes distortion of economic policies - is more difficult to recognize. It is difficult to differentiate between deliberately-chosen-damaging-but-self-serving (for the policy makers) policies and poor economic policy making. Economists seem to have had - until recently - difficulties with modeling such behavior. The objective of this book is to stimulate further studies on corruption by providing a review of the existing work in this field and raising some questions that need to be addressed. Contributors to this volume will attempt to synthesize studies dealing with various aspects of corruption and bring together some new questions that have been raised about the origin and impact of corruption.

In this book we elaborates upon the following issues that have been raised in an attempt to understand corruption. What is corruption and how can it be defined? How can we model corruption? How can the extent of corruption in a society be measured? What are its consequences? What other economic activities does corruption influence? How can we measure the effects of corruption on these activities? Why does it continue to exist, that is, the political economy of corruption? What can be done about it? Given the importance of market-orientation in contemporary economic policy making, it may be worthwhile to ask if such reforms cause or cure corruption (Kaufmann 1997).

This book may be divided into three parts. The next two chapters build a framework for understanding corruption. The following two chapters deal with empirical issues - measurement of corruption and its effects. The last two chapters of the book move in the direction of action: what can be done, what cannot be done.

Earlier in this chapter we had identified two reasons why it is so difficult to study corruption. These difficulties are compounded by many levels at which corruption occurs. In the chapters that follow in this book, two very different types of corruption are being identified and discussed. The image that the word "corruption" conjures in the minds of most people is one of bribery - if you have to pay someone under the table, there is corruption. It is the type of corruption in which it is possible to say that a government official is using his/her administrative power for personal gains. It is easy to recognize when this type of corruption occurs - even if it is very difficult to measure it. This type of corruption is usually called administrative or bureaucratic corruption. Most of the recent work in economics has focused on this type of corruption. Many of the models of this type of corruption are summarized in chapter 2. In the chapter titled

"Corruption in Comparative Perception" Lambsdorff discusses attempts to measure this type of corruption and some problems that can arise in using these measures for empirical analysis.

The second type of corruption is more difficult to define and identify. Its impact, however, may be far greater than that of the administrative corruption. We refer here to what is generally known as political corruption. A politician may base resource allocation decision not on the criteria of public welfare but on who may benefit from the decision. The politician may circumvent the acceptable procedure for making resource allocation decisions - giving rise to the most insidious type of corruption. The problem in identifying this type of corruption is that most public decisions are based on multiple, and often conflicting, criteria. Attribution of the decision to one criteria alone requires proof that only the decision makers possess but are unlikely to provide. This type of corruption is described in terms of the corruption of the political elite in the second chapter. The difficulties in measuring this type of corruption as well as its consequences, however, are best illustrated by Naylor in his descriptions of how the arms business works.

Attempts to solve corruption have to begin with the level at which corruption exists and the type of corruption that is considered to be the most serious and the important corruption. Clearly what may work in one situation may not in the other. Assume that a political leader decided that corruption in the country must be removed or at least reduced. If, as Tanzi argues, the corruption has spread in a cancel like fashion to all organizations and throughout the society, this leader is unlikely to receive the cooperation of bureaucrats who will have to play an important role in combating corruption. If the previous regime was marked by corruption at all levels, chances are that the bureaucracy has developed working relationships with those who need the bureaucracies. These users and the bureaucrats have probably created a set of rules by which they interact with each other - including rules about who has to be paid and how much for which activity. More important, corruption has probably come to be accepted in the society and everyone has come to rely upon it to obtain what they need. What can the new corruption-fighting leader do to reduce the level of corruption in such a society? The approach that this leader has to take is probably very different from one who is trying to reduce corruption in a society where corruption is not widespread and is not seen as a legitimate activity. The two last chapters in the book attempt to address these issues.

The chapter on "Models of Corruption" begins with an attempt to define corruption. Since most of the corruption that we encounter revolves around the role of government - either of the politicians or of the bureaucrats - an attempt to made in that chapter to identify all the relationships between various parts of the government and their clients. Using the principal-agent framework, various relationships in which one or the other part of government acts as an agent are identified. This framework is used in the later part of the chapter to summarize various models of corruption that have been proposed. Before various models of corruption are summarized, however, an attempt has been made to differentiate between exertion of influence to obtain favors or economic benefits that may be considered legitimate and exertion of influence which can be labeled as corruption or rent seeking. Models of corruption are divided into two main groups. Much of the past work in this area has framed the problem in terms of rent seeking behavior. Models of rent seeking behavior analyze the problem in terms of effects on the resource allocation in the economy. The clear conclusion of these models is that since rent seeking behavior does not contribute to the production of goods and services, it is welfare reducing. Rent seeking models, however, miss an important point about the relationship between those who seek to enhance their returns from their assets and those who hold legislative controls: assets holders can make side payments to achieve their goals - leading to corruption. Models of corruption have generally been proposed within the agency theoretic framework. In chapter 2, these models have been separated into those explaining legislative or political corruption and those explaining administrative or bureaucratic corruption. The final section of the chapter attempts to identify some questions about the political economy of the corruption: why are the markets not able to take care of eliminating corruption?

R. T. Naylor, in his chapter on the corruption in the arms business, reminds us that the eradication of corruption requires more than passing laws that declare the activity illegal. Corruption exists in an historical and cultural context. What is considered acceptable and unacceptable depends upon what has happened in the past. Naylor starts with the assumption that business transactions are motivated by greed. Hence people making these transactions will try to find ways to increase their profits. Naylor's most important point is that these attempts will be successful, regardless of what the existing legal code says, if those at the helm of affairs in a country agree with these motives. There could be two reasons why the decision making elite agrees with the "anything-goes-as-long-as-profits-are-made" attitude: either these profit making activities are also in the interest of the society as a whole or the elite derives some economic benefits from these decisions. Naylor shows quite convincingly that, at least in the arms business, it is the second reason that dominates. Hence his conclusion that fighting corruption requires more than a change in laws. Naylor points to some specific difficulties we are likely to face in fighting corruption in this industry. First, this industry consists of deeply entrenched constituencies - industrial firms and the military. Second, the military might and culture makes it difficult and even dangerous for investigators to carry out their work. In the arms business, however, Naylor points out that corruption may actually work in the interest of the global society in that corruption and excessive profits result in fewer arms being sold for a given size of procurement budgets. This benefit, however, may disappear if the same motivation - for excess profits - succeeds in influencing the sizes of the budgets.

The subsequent chapter, "Corruption: Quantitative Estimates," attempts to familiarize the reader with the wide variety of techniques and methodologies that have been used to measure the impact and extent of corruption. There is a long history of studies on rent seeking behavior whereas studies on corruption are of recent vintage. In the past, scholars had focused on specific acts of corruption. Since these acts tend not to be publicized and recorded, empirical estimates were found to be difficult. Over the last few years, however, scholars have successfully modeled macroeconomic consequences of corruption and begin to measure the validity of these models. The aim of the chapter is to present the variety of methodologies to researchers who may be unfamiliar with the growing literature in this field. Since most of the empirical work is also closely linked to the measurement of corruption, some empirical studies have been summarized in Chapter 5. A summary of those studies has not been included in Chapter 4.

Chapter 5 by Johann Graf Lambsdorff introduces readers to one aspect of the work of Transparency International (TI), Berlin. TI has carried out perhaps the first systematic study to measure corruption around the world using the same yardstick for every country. In his chapter titled "Corruption in Comparative Perception," Lambsdorff first reviews some of the past studies in that have used some measure of corruption and then discusses some problems with the measures used in those studies. He then goes on to outline TI's approach for the measurement of a corruption index and the results of this effort. The actual index, included in an appendix to the chapter, is analyzed by the author as to the perception of various groups of contributors to the index. Potential users of this index will find this description very useful since it allows us to estimate the nature of compromises that had to be made in creating the index.

Vito Tanzi begins the process of addressing the question of what has to be done about corruption in his chapter on the effects of corruption on government budgets. He tackles a number of important issues regarding the relationship between corruption and government activities. Whether or not increased government's involvement in a society leads to higher corruption depends upon circumstances. Tanzi discusses various types of corrupt activities that evolve under different circumstances and how these activities have different impact on the economic growth. Corruption is also practiced differently in different branches of government. It, therefore, follows that attempts to reduce corruption will have to take into account where, how, and why corrupt activities exist. In the concluding section of the chapter, the author emphasizes the need for a commitment of the leadership as well as a change in the environment that are needed to resolve the problem.

In the final chapter in this book, Kaufmann presents concrete ideas on what direction future research in this area may have to take and about how corruption can be tackled. After reviewing existing definitions and causes of corruption, the author makes a very important contribution by providing a typology of corruption. Empirical research in this area has hitherto not been able to distinguish, partly for reasons of availability of data and partly for lack of conceptual clarity, between various types of activities that fall under the umbrella of corruption. By providing a mapping of various activities and their characteristics, Kaufmann has laid the grounds for research on corruption to move to a higher level: we will refine this typology and begin to look separately at causes, consequences, and remedies for various types of corruption. Throughout the chapter, the author has recommendations for where further research may be of value in enhancing our understanding of corruption. Finally, his perspective of an "operationally-oriented research economist" is useful guide on what can be done to reduce corruption.

It is hoped that this book provides a review of a wide variety of topics relating to corruption. Readers of this book may notice one omission. There are no country studies in this book. This omission has been deliberate. Although case studies of countries or specific instances of corruption provide very useful insights in to how corruption travels through economic and political systems, they do not allow for generalizations. The aim of this book is to show that corruption matters regardless of the situation or the country, and to stimulate further studies on this subject.

ACKNOWLEDGEMENTS

The author is grateful to the Social Sciences and Humanities Research Council, Ottawa, for a grant that made this research possible.

NOTES

[1] Leiken measures this by the number of articles mentioning corruption in selected publications (1997: 58). He reports that this number in 1995 has quadrupled since 1984. The increase in this number, however, could reflect merely greater propensity to report corruption as compared to the past. Also see Mauro (1998).

[2] See Tanzi (1995: 7) for a similar view.

[3] Some of the exceptions include the limited literature on rent seeking in addition to such works as Rose-Ackerman 1978.

[4] Kurer (1993: 262-3) cites a number of studies that point very clearly to the influence of corruption on the types of decisions made by the politicians. He also shows how the neglect of the importance of corruption in view of this evidence is rationalized.

[5] An exception may be the analysis of the crisis in East Asia in 1997-98. While discussing the possibilities of the tiger economies finding their ways through the crisis, the Economist emphasized the difficulties some of these countries may face due to corruption within the countries (Economist, 1998).

[6] See Ackerman 1978, Collander 1984, Shleifer and Vishny 1992 and 1993, Murphy, Shleifer and Vishny 1991 and 1993, Jain 1993, Krueger 1993, Tanzi 1995 for some of the discussions regarding these effects.

[7] Tanzi, 1995, points out that corruption undermines the tax policy of the government as well as the effectiveness of government stabilization policies. Tanzi and Davoodi, 1997, provide empirical support for this.

[8] Shleifer and Vishny (1993: 599). Shleifer and Vishny, however, go on to discuss consequences of far more serious forms of corruption. Tanzi, 1995, provides a detailed definition from Indian Penal Code that takes this view of corruption.

[9] The term "rent seeking" was coined by Krueger, 1974, and the term "directly unproductive profit-seeking" activities by Bhagwati, 1980. For a recent review of the work on these activities, see Tullock, 1993.

[10] The payments associated with corruption do not seem to be that high in comparison with the costs and benefits of corruption. As discussed above, payments of around $15000 each to 29 politicians result in losses for consumers that run into billions of dollars in the case of sugar industry in the United States.

[11] See, among others, references to the works of Bardhan 1997, Elliot (1997), Kaufmann 1997, Shleifer and Vishny 1993, - some of whose work is with Murphy 1991, and 1993, Tanzi 1995, Mauro 1995, and 1997. A number of attempts have been made to develop quantitative estimates of corruption during the past few years. Some of these attempts will be reviewed in the subsequent chapters in this book.

[12] The president of the World Bank introduced this concern at the joint annual meeting of the Bank and the International Monetary Fund in 1996. The issue was discussed at great lengths at the annual meeting of 1997.

REFERENCES

Bardhan, Pranab. (1997). "Corruption and Development: A Review of Issues." *Journal Of Economic Literature*, 35: 1320-1346.

Cameron, Stevie. (1994). *On The Take: Crime, Corruption, And Greed In The Mulroney Years*, Toronto: MacFarlane Walter and Ross.

Collander, David C., (Ed.) (1984). *Neoclassical Political Economy: The Analysis of Rent-seeking and DUP Activities*, Mass.: Ballinger publishing Co.

Committee on Foreign Affairs. (1984). "The Mexican Economic Crisis: Policy Implications for the United States." House of Representatives, 98th congress, Washington DC.

Dornbusch, Rudiger, and Sebastian Edwards, (eds.) (1991). *The Macroeconomics of Populism in Latin America*. Chicago: University of Chicago press.

Economist, The. (1998). "Frozen Miracle: A Survey of East Asian Economies." *The Economist*, March 7.

Elliot, Kimberly Ann. (Ed.) (1997). *Corruption and the Global Economy*. Washington DC: Institute for International Economics.

Jain, Arvind K. (1993). "Dictatorships, Democracies, and Debt Crisis." In S. P. Riley, (ed.), *The Politics Of Global Debt*, New York: St. Martin's Press.

Johnson, Simon, Daniel Kaufmann, and Pablo Zoido-Lobaton. (1998). "Regulatory Discretion and the Unofficial Economy." *American Economic Review*, 88: 387-392.

Kaufmann, Daniel. (1997). "Economic Corruption: The Facts," *Foreign Policy*, 107 (Summer): 114-31.

Klitgaard, Robert. (1990). *Tropical Gangsters*, New York: Basic Books.

Krueger, Anne Osborne. (1974). "The Political Economy of the Rent-Seeking Society," *American Economic Review*, 64: 291-303.

_____. (1993). *Political Economy Of Policy Reform In Developing Countries*, Mass: MIT press.

Kurer, Oskar. (1993). "Clientelism, Corruption, and the Allocation of Resources," *Public Choice*, 77(2): 259-273.

Leiken, Robert S. (1997). "Controlling the Global Corruption Epidemic," *Foreign Policy*, no. 105: 55-76.

Mauro, Paolo. (1995). "Corruption and Growth," *Quarterly Journal of Economics*, 110(3): 681-712.

_____. (1997). "The Effects of Corruption on Growth, Investment, and Government Expenditure: A Cross–Country Analysis." In Kimberly Ann Elliot (ed.), *Corruption and the Global Economy*, Washington D.C.: Institute for International Economics, pp. 83–107.

_____. (1998). "Corruption: Cuases, Consequences, and Agenda for Further Research," *Finance and Development*, 35 (1): 11-14.

Murphy, Kevin, M., Andrei Shleifer and Robert Vishny. (1991). "The Allocation of Talent: Implications for Growth." *Quarterly Journal of Economics*, 106: 503-30.

_____. (1993). "Why is Rent-Seeking so Costly to Growth?" *American Economic Review*, 82(2): 409-414.

Naylor, R.T. (1987). *Hot Money and The Politics of Debt.* Toronto: McClelland and Stewart.

Rose-Ackerman, Susan. (1978). *Corruption: A Study In Political Economy.* Academic Press.

Shleifer, Andrei and Robert Vishny. (1992). "Pervasive Shortages Under Socialism," *RAND Journal of Economics*, 23(2): 237-246.

_____. (1993). "Corruption." *Quarterly Journal Of Economics*, 108(3): 99-617.

Stackhouse, John. (1994). "Public-Service Jobs Provide Key to Mint." *Globe And Mail*, December 30: A1, A7.

Tanzi, Vito and Partho Shome. (1993). "A Primer on Tax Evasion." *IMF Staff Papers*, 40(4): 807-828.

Tanzi, Vito, 1995. "Corruption, Government Activities, and Markets." In Gianluca Fiorentini and Sam Petzman (eds.), *The Economics of Organized Crime*, Cambridge: Cambridge University Press.

Tanzi, V. and Davoodi, H. (1997). "Corruption, Public Investment, and Growth." IMF Working Paper WP/97/139.

Tullock, Gordon. (1993). *Rent Seeking*, The Shaftesbury papers, 2, U.K.: Hants Edward Elgar.

2
MODELS OF CORRUPTION

ARVIND K. JAIN
Concordia University

WHAT IS CORRUPTION?

How can corruption be defined? What are the different types of corruption? What, if any, is the distinction between rent-seeking and corruption? What do we include in our definition, what do we exclude?

Almost everyone who writes about corruption attempts to first define it. Some of prominent surveys include those by Heidenheimer (1970, especially pp 3-28 and Chapter 1), Rose-Ackerman (1978), and Colander (1984). Almost all recognize that it is difficult to do so given the broad range of activities that could be included under the rubric of corruption. One can give examples that others will agree involve corruption. These examples cover patronage appointments, bribery, misuse of authority and power, and favoritism in awarding contracts.[1] Johnston (1982) provides a typology of various types of political corruption. Some prefer a subjective(or even tautological) definition: "corruption is what is called corruption" (Brasz 1970: 43). By and large, all these definitions center around derivation of economic benefits from institutional power inherent in political and bureaucratic appointments. Many recognize that corruption involves personal relationships and may even represent informal markets where formal ones have either failed or been circumvented.[2]

To understand the relationship between various definitions of corruption, we extend the principal-agent model that is frequently used in economics. We want to understand the relationship between government leaders who make policies and appoint bureaucrats, bureaucrats who implement these policies, firms that produce economic goods, and the populace whose welfare depends, at least partly, upon what the other three do.

We call the populace the clients C_1, C_2 ... C_n. These clients appoint the government leaders, A_0, as their general agent to manage the economy.[3] This agent regulates the environment under which privately-owned-profit-maximizing organizations S_1 ... S_j, produce goods and services for the economy. This regulations determines the profits that these organizations would be able to earn. The agent also controls the budget that determines government's purchases of services from these organizations. The private organizations are owned by some of the clients C_{k+1} .. C_{k+p} such that p << n. The agent, A_0, also appoints, as agents, the bureaucrats A_1 ... A_{m-j} who manage organizations S_{j+1} ... S_m which may be seen as various government agencies providing unique services to the public. These relationships are outlined in Exhibit 2.1.

The clients C_1 ... C_n want the agent A_0 to look after their interests and to maximize their welfare. Some of the clients who own the profit maximizing organizations S_1 ... S_j will have to balance their conflicting objectives - those as members of the populace and those as owners of these profit making organizations. We assume, however, that their objectives as producers dominate their objectives as members of the general population. All the agents, A_0 as well as A_1 ... A_{m-j}, are assumed to maximize their own welfare rather than be pathologically honest towards their principals.[4]

There are at least three relationships in this framework that concern us. The first two are principal-agent relationships, one between the clients C_1 ... C_n and the agent A_0 and the other between the agent A_0 and the agents A_1 ... A_{m-j}, and the third is the relationship between the agents A_1 ... A_{m-j} and the clients C_1 ... C_n. All three of these relationships are fraught with difficulties.[5] There are incentives for all the agents to ignore the interests of their principals and maximize their own welfare at the cost of these principals. Consider first the relationship between the agent A_0 and its principals.

The profits of the organizations S_1 ... S_j depend, among other things, on their ability to acquire assets with monopolistic rents. In classical economic thinking, these rents would not exist due to competition. Modern analysis, however, recognizes that such competition does not always work at least partly due to rent seeking or directly unproductive profit-seeking, or DUP, activities (Colander 1984). Economic entities do not passively accept erosion of their monopoly powers. The profit maximizing organizations will attempt, among other things, to influence the regulations that the agent A_0 tries to introduce. There are at least three ways in which they will invest resources to protect and enhance these monopoly positions. The route they choose will have consequences for the welfare of principal ($\{C_1$ ... $C_n\}$ - $\{C_{k+1}$ ... $C_{k+p}\}$) and for the level of corruption in the economy.

Exhibit 2.1

SOME PRINCIPAL - AGENT RELATIONSHIPS IN AN ECONOMY

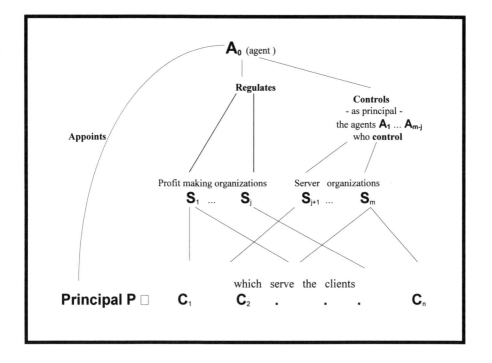

(i) They can invest resources in technology needed to develop the monopolistic advantage. Owners of such technology benefit from it till the time the technology is copied by its competitors.

When a holder of monopoly power acquires that position without influencing the regulatory process, except through an open public debate, we view it as developing competitive strength. Any rent extracted from such a position is viewed as a legitimate reward for building a monopolistic (or competitive) position within a market system. This Schumpeterian view of monopoly power is consistent with criterion of economic efficiency.[6]

(ii) Engage in directly unproductive profit-seeking activities within the rules of the game - that is - in a manner that is open to competition. These rules include possibility to influence government policy through purchase of politicians.[7] These activities may include " ... 'tariff-seeking' lobbying, tariff evasion, and premium seeking for given import licenses..." (Bhagwati, Brecher, and Srinivasan, 1984: 18).[8]

For such an influence not to be seen as involving corruption, the above transactions between the agent A_0 and the organizations S_1 ... S_j must be arms-length transactions. Any input that the property holders have in the regulatory process has to be transparent and provided within a system where the contestants for the asset, and owners of contesting assets, have equal access to the regulators. There would be no side payments from the asset holders to the regulators in this situation. These transactions may or may not be welfare enhancing: "These activities are 'rent-seeking' in the sense that the resources devoted to obtaining the item of value do not create value and constitute a dead-weight cost" (Krueger 1993: 58).[9]

(iii) Engage in what will also be called rent seeking or directly unproductive profit-seeking activities, but do so outside the rules of the game. These activities could include influencing A_0 who is responsible for enactment of regulations that create monopoly rents for the designated assets. The agent may agree to such regulations even though they are not in the interests of its principal, C_1 ... C_n and may charge a price if it agrees to be influenced.[10] The extent of monopoly created by regulation determines the potential rent, and hence the price that the agent may charge, associated with the regulatory power. These activities may create information asymmetry and may even be illegal.

The last situation requires a collusion between the clients C_{k+1} ... C_{k+p} and the agent A_0. What differentiates the third situation from the second is the extent of information that is revealed to the principal ($\{C_1 \ldots C_n\}$ - $\{C_{k+1} \ldots C_{k+p}\}$). Under the second alternative, the transaction is transparent and all the participants have full information about the activities of the agent. Under the third alternative, however, the manner of influence or collusion is either not revealed to the principal or is in contravention of the (implicit or explicit) contract by which the agent was employed, or both. The principal, if it were to make the decision itself, would not approve of such a collusion. In addition, the agent, in most cases, will demand some form of compensation from the organization that benefits from the collusion.

This situation has potential for the most serious type of corruption. Organizations $S_1 \ldots S_j$ have incentive to influence A_0 to pass regulation that will increase their rents. They would be willing to pay a part of this excess rent to the agent. If the agent A_0's expected cost of accepting these payments do not exceed the value of these payments, it will agree to pass legislation that favors $S_1 \ldots S_j$ at the cost of $\{C_1 \ldots C_n\}$ - $\{C_{k+1} \ldots C_{k+p}\}$. As the agent's cost of these payments goes down, as it would under an agent that has full control of the legislative and administrative instruments of the society, corruption will increase. When the payments associated with accepting corruption related payments are high, the agent A_0 may have to find ways to legitimize changing regulation or budgetary decisions that will allow it to earn the corrupt income.[11] This type of corruption involves agent A_0's use, for personal gains, of the executive and legislative powers that it has been delegated. In extreme cases, this agent may even own some of the organizations $S_1 \ldots S_j$, thus obviating side payments.

The second agency relationship arises between A_0 (as the principal) and $A_1 \ldots A_{m-j}$ (as the agents). This relationship meets the requirements for a classic information-asymmetry based agency problem. Agents $A_1 \ldots A_{m-j}$ have incentives to extract more benefits from their control of the organization $S_1 \ldots S_j$, shirk work, and even re-orient the goals of these organizations.

Next consider incentives faced by the agents $A_1 \ldots A_{m-j}$ in their relationship with $C_1 \ldots C_n$ - the third relationship of interest to us. By our definition, each of these agents has a monopoly over the services it provides to the public.[12] These agents may threaten to increase the transaction cost associated with a service by slowing down the process - even making the cost infinite if the service can be denied. They may then charge a rent for speeding up the process - thus lowering the transaction cost from what it could be. In extreme case, the agents may even have the abilities to let the applicant escape the regulations entirely. These actions are rarely sanctioned by law but are costly to monitor.[13] Ability to manipulate this power gives rise to the most common forms of petty corruption.

We can thus identify two situations that can be labeled as constituting corruption. The first is a simple case of misappropriation of government property - often called administrative corruption. The second is misuse of power to make decisions which change the profile of returns on various assets in the economy - often called political corruption.[14] Most instances of corruption would seem to fall between the two extremes described above - actions of the agent A_0 where it is able to change the returns associated with various assets in the economy, and the actions of the agents A_1... A_{m-j} who are able to charge a price for providing a service for which they have already been compensated in other forms.

In this framework, corruption seems to require three elements. First, someone has monopolistic power over a process - the process being design of some regulation or delivery of some government services. Second this individual is willing and able to misuse that power. Third, there is economic incentive for the misuse of power.

Whether power can be seen as being misused or not would seem to depend upon the circumstances surrounding the process as well as the relationship between the clients on one hand and the agents on the other. This process is recognized as free of corruption if all of the following three conditions are met.[15] (i) It represents a competitive game played under rules known to all the players, (ii) there are no secret or side payments to the agent, and (iii) the clients and the agents are independent of each other in the sense that none of these benefits from income earned by the other. If any of these three conditions is violated, the process acquires characteristics of corruption.

These conditions would seem to rules out much of the rent seeking behavior from being labeled as corruption. The second condition limits corruption to those activities where the agent expects some returns from the transaction - how so ever imprecisely measured and regardless of the time period over which the benefit is received. The third condition recognizes the importance of parochial corruption (Scott 1970) or the building of "social capital" (for example, "guanxi" in China, Tanzi 1995) through misuse of power.

The manners in which an agent can misuse its powers and create situations of corruption seems to lead to a definition of corruption that is an extension of the one offered by Shleifer and Vishny (1993: 599.) Although their definition covers all situations where the agent allows some one else to extract the monopoly rents from assets allocated by the government, it may not cover situations where the agent expropriates assets for itself. We define corruption as manipulation of powers of government or sale of government property, or both, by government officials for personal use.

It may be worthwhile to understand how rent-seeking differs from corruption.[16] The main difference seems to be that law generally permits rent-seeking activities whereas corruption usually involves activities that are illegal. Buchanan provides a basic definition of rent: "Rent is that part of the payment to an owner of resources over and above that which those resources could command in any alternative use" (1980: 3). He seems to equate - in this definition - rent seeking to profit seeking. They both result from the same activity of an individual - the owner of the resources - who is trying to maximize the value of these resources. The difference is in unintended consequences: consequences of profit maximization are socially desirable whereas those of rent seeking are wasteful.

Tullock provides a definition similar to Buchanan. "... (A)n individual who invests in something that will not actually improve productivity or will actually lower it, but that does raise his income because it gives him some special position or monopoly power, is 'rent seeking'..." (1980: 17). Tullock (1993: 22) raises issues of what is corruption and recognizes that it is certainly not investing resources in legitimate activities such as research etc. which then yield rents.

MODELS AND CONSEQUENCES

The second part of the chapter provides a framework to link the wide range of models that have been used to explain corruption as well as rent seeking and to assess its consequences. What are the objectives of these models? What do these models assume about the behavior of various actors? What kind of equilibrium is achieved with the above assumptions? What are the consequences of corruption? In discussing these issues we do not, at least for the time being, distinguish between corruption and rent seeking.

Broadly, models of corruption or rent seeking take one of two approaches. First set of models, which can be labelled as resource allocation models for convenience, treat these activities like any other resource-absorbing activity in an economy. These model assess the consequences of allocation of resources to rent seeking activities - activities requiring input of labor and subject to a production function. Pure rent seeking models in the tradition of Krueger (1974), Bhagwati (1982), Buchanan, Tollison, and Tullock (1980), or Tullock (1993), concern themselves with the implications of allocation of resources to rent seeking activities, especially with the prices of the assets and their returns. In these models, rent seeking activities compete with productive activities for resources.

Second group of models employ, explicitly or implicitly, the principal-agent relationships to explain corruption. These models focus on the actions of a corrupt agent - agents that engage in "the misuse of public power for private profit or political gain" (Leiken 1997: 55; agents A_0 as well as A_1 ... A_{m-j} in Exhibit 1) under the constraints that can be imposed by their principals. The principal-agent models may be further separated into two groups. The vast majority of these models refer to the relationship between the government leaders, A_0, and the bureaucrats, A_1 ... A_{m-j}, and attribute the agency problem to information asymmetry which results from the principal's inability to monitor the agent's behavior (Rose-Ackerman 1978, for example) or even to set measurable goals. Only a few of these models see the agency problem arising due to lack of control - situations in which the principal lacks the means to replace, or to exercise full control, over the agent. A few authors, relying on informal descriptions, show how a corrupt agent A_0 can make self-serving economic as well as political decisions which may not be in the interest of the principal and the principal is unable to do something about it (Klitgaard 1990, 1991, Kurer 1993, Jain 1988, 1993).

More recent models, for example by Shleifer and Vishny (1993) and Tanzi (1995), and empirical tests by Mauro (1995), combine the two approaches used to construct the models of corruption. These models are able to examine the incentives for the agents to be corrupt, effects of the agents' corruption on other economic activities, most notably the entrepreneurial activities, and hence the implications for resource allocation within general equilibrium model of the economy.

Consequences of corruption can be distinguished according to their immediate and subsequent impacts on the economy. Some types of corruption cause - *primarily* - income redistribution whereas other types cause - *primarily* - misallocation of resources. Study of the consequences of corruption is complicated because in general equilibrium framework each of these effects will most likely lead to the other effect as well. Thus, income redistribution will lead to a change in the pattern of allocation of resources and misallocation of resources will cause income redistribution.

Study of the consequences of corruption becomes even more complicated if it is assumed that decision-makers internalize cost of corruption in their decision making process. Decision-makers could anticipate costs of corruption and their resource allocation decisions would reflect their estimates of post-corruption resource costs. In such cases, it would be difficult to measure the full costs of corruption by examining merely the outcomes of corrupt acts.

Bearing these difficulties of examining the literature on corruption, we review the most important models of corruption.

Resource Allocation Models

The underlying theme of most of the rent seeking analysis is based on "...individuals' attempts to escape the invisible hand of the market and to redirect policy proposals for their own advantage. Whereas traditional neoclassical welfare economics assumes government to be an exogenous force, trying to do good, new neoclassical political economists argue that government is at least partially endogenous and the policies it institutes will reflect vested interests in society" (Colander 1984: 2).[17] For the traditional "perfectly competitive equilibrium" to be stable, "... all individuals would need to accept passively the institutions and government policies upon which it is based. If, however, the marginal gain from changing the institution is less than the marginal gain from maintaining it, that competitive equilibrium will not be stable, .." (Colander 1984: 3). Thus, rent seeking models are based on the premise that "rent seeking is one part of an economic activity, such as distribution or production, and part of the firm's resources are devoted to the activity (including, of course, the hiring of expediters)" (Krueger 1974: 293). The rent seeking model can also be applied to activities of different bureaucracies competing for budgets (Faith, 1980).

Resource allocation models of rent seeking assume a competitive world in which entreprenuers (and labor) have a choice of spending their efforts on production of goods and services or on rent seeking activities. Prices for goods, services, and labor are determined by the market but the government allocates licenses to produce (or import) goods and services. Entreprenuers compete with each other to obtain these licenses. The underlying assumption in these models is that rent seeking activities require resources but do not affect the costs of production of goods or services; they merely re-direct the right to produce them from one entreprenuer to another. As such, rent seeking activities do not add to the welfare of the society.[18]

Under these assumptions, it is not surprising that these models prove that rent seeking activities result in a net loss for the economy. If playing a zero-sum games is going to require resources, welfare losses are to be expected. In her seminal paper, Krueger showed that "rent seeking entails a welfare loss beyond that for an import restriction without rent seeking" (1974: 299).

Krueger estimated costs of rent seeking for India and Turkey. The most important category reported by her is that for import licenses. It appears that these licenses cost about 5% of the national income in India in 1964 and about 15 percent of the GNP in Turkey in 1968 (p. 294). Similar conclusions are drawn by almost all the authors who have extended the basic rent seeking models. More recently, Lenway, Morck and Yeung

(1996) have estimated the consequences of rent seeking in the steel industry in the United States for employees, managers and the economy. The managers who engage in rent seeking are found to improve their earnings at the cost of the other two groups.

Costs of rent seeking can also be measured indirectly. Katz and Rosenberg (1994) measure the consequences of rent seeking for the budgets of the central government, ignoring any other rent seeking in a country. They find that "(a) (E)very *change* in the proportion of the government's budget spent for a given purpose occurs as a result of rent seeking activity by pressure groups" and "(b) (T)he aggregate dollar value of the resources wasted by all competitors to achieve changes in government's budgetary allocation is equal to the dollar amount of the change in the budgetary allocation." Mixon, Laband and Ekelund examined the possibilities that those seeking favors offer politicians meals. They find that state capital cities in the United States contain more restaurants that allow clients to offer politicians in-kind payments, through meals, rather than cash and argue that their finding is "compatible with greater resource distortion that is openly observed" (1994: 173).

Extensions of the simple models of rent seeking follow at least two routes. Application of game theory shows how firms will behave when there is competition for rent seeking or when they can cooperate with each other (Linster 1994). The general conclusion of these models would appear to be that "the extent of aggregate rent seeking, and hence the total social cost of seeking rent, is determined by the rent available to capture,..., and the number of players in the game" (Paul and Wilhite, 1994: 110). The second set of studies examine the effects of rent seeking on the market structure. It is possible to ask if rent seeking activities end up influencing market equilibrium through their effects on the cost of resources. Analysis indicates that firms spending resources on rent seeking activities end up being less efficient than those that do not spend such resources under certain conditions (Zhou 1995, Lenway, Morck and Yeung, 1996).[19]

Agency Models of Corruption

By far the most frequently used models of corruption rely upon the agency theory. The problems in the principal-agent relationship between the populace and the government leaders (agent A_0) arise from the misuse of the legislative powers held by the agent. This agency problem is modelled only infrequently although its importance is recognized by many.[20] We define legislative corruption as that arising from the misuse of legislative powers by government - democratic or otherwise - in power. We define bureaucratic corruption as that arising from the agency relationship between the leaders and the bureaucrats, that is, between agent A_0 on the one hand and the agents A_1 ... A_{m-j} on the other. Most models of corruption focus on the bureaucratic corruption (Rose-Ackerman 1978, Shleifer and Vishny 1993, Tanzi 1995).

Legislative Corruption

According to the schematic introduced in Exhibit 1, the agent A_0 has the authority to regulate the environment in which the server organizations, S_1 ... S_j operate as well as the authority - legislative - to appoint the agents A_1 ... A_{m-j}. We define legislative corruption as arising from misuse of these powers by the agent A_0. Studies of this type of corruption may be divided according to the motives attributed to the agent A_0. Many studies of legislative corruption focus on the desire of the legislator to be re-elected. Others recognize that this agent may seek economic benefits from its poistion and design policies that increase that benefit (Kurer 1993, Lien 1990). A small number of authors have focused on the legislative corruption in its extreme form in which the agent is able to undermine all controls of the principal and is able to maximize benefits for itself (Klitgaard 1990, 1991, Jain 1988, 1993).

There is long tradition in economics and political science of questioning the motives of legislators. Clearly they are influenced by bribes and side payments. A number of studies in Heidenheimer (1970) describe behavior of politicians under these circumstances. Rose-Ackerman (1978, chapters 2-4) elaborates on these issues. Most of these models, however, focus on the desire of the legislator to be reelected. Motivation for reelection is the "political income" (Barro 1973) over and above the contracted income. Equilibrium in these models depends upon how the elected agents balance the interests or the payments of various interest groups that want to influence the legislation against the welfare of the voters (Barro 1973, Becker 1983, Grossman and Helpman, 1994).

Lien (1990) develops a model when this agent accepts bribes, and discriminates in the favor of some firms that are bidding for the project. The discrimination, which exagerates the effects of bribes, is not motivated by financial rewards over and above the bribe, but may result from considerations of friendships. Lien shows that in a situation of uncertaintly, that is, when firms do not know each others' cost functions, and hence their propensities to bribe, decision of a corrupt agent will result in projects being awarded to firms that are not the most efficient. Kurer (1993) with the help of a model in which policy makers are corrupt, refutes the argument that corruption may actually bring about efficiency by mitigating the effects of poor economic policies. As shown by his model, the efficiency benefits of corruption disappear when corruption is endogenous to the model.

A subset of models that explain legislative corruption may be termed as "dictatorship models of corruption" (Klitgaard, 1990, 1991, Jain 1988, 1993) or models of a "totalitarian socialism" (Shleifer and Vishny, 1994). These models view policy makers as agents who are able to ignore the interests of their principals almost completely.[21] Such an approach challenges the existing economic orthodoxy which assumes that "...government actions are the responses of policymakers to sociopolitical pressure brought to bear upon them by interest groups." (Frieden, 199: 5-6) - an approach which is at least more sophisticated than the older assumption that governments are "benevolent social guardian" (a term used by Krueger1993). Dictatorship models assume that the form of the government can be the predatory, as described by Lal-Myint (referenced in Krueger, 1993, page 60).

The dictatorship models of legislative corruption are based on two premises. First, like the other agency models, agents are assumed to maximize their own welfare. Second, they are assumed to be able to eliminate, or at least significantly decrease the impact of, the threats of actions by the principal that could constrain the agent's behavior. Following this self interest can lead the decision makers to indulge in corrupt behavior. The hypothesis of these models is that the distortion caused by the role of agent - who is assumed (or defined) as being corrupt - significantly changes the economic policy from what it would be if the behavior of the agent would be fully controlled. Economic policies motivated by the self interests of the policy makers may lead to immediate misallocation of resources. This will result simultaneously in loss of income and redistribution of income. Corruption, in this case, benefits the policy maker in the form of kickbacks or income for related parties. Misallocation of resources can also be caused by a distortion of incentives faced by investors in the society. Distortion of these incentives, in turn, causes further misallocation of resources. This consequence appears to be similar to the misallocation of resources when rent seeking or directly unproductive activities become one of the alternatives that individuals follow.

Legislative corruption will cause misallocation of resources when the choice of projects is governed by A_0's payoff associated with each project. The agent's desire to extract the highest possible rent distorts the decisions that is made because some decisions yield higher rent than others for the decision maker (Lien 1990).

This can be illustrated with an example. A_0 has the authority to decide which projects will be undertaken. Client C_i is going to implement the project and expects to earn a return from this project. There may be many project and only one of these will be chosen. There are many C_i's competing for each project. Each C_i is willing to pay a price to obtain the contract. A kickback is expected by A_0 which could take the form of profit sharing or appointment of A_0's associates to position in the project. A_0's choice of project in this situation will be determined by the level of payoffs associated with each project, not by the value of the project for the principal. When this types of corruption has been institutionalized, it may lead to the development of a market for public office (Wade 1985).

Bureaucratic Corruption.

Models of bureaucratic corruption follow the usual line of analysis of agency theory. Agents have incentives to disregard their principal's interest due to information asymmetry. The principal lacks ability to monitor the agent's behavior because monitoring is costly. In the absence of perfect information, the principal must design incentive contracts that encourage the agent to maximize the principal's welfare.

Shleifer and Vishny (1993) offer a comprehensive model of the behavior of government officials A_1, A_2,... A_{m-j} under various assumptions regarding their relationship with A_0 and under various market conditions. Comparing the marginal returns to corruption for these officials, the authors conclude that "corruption with theft (when the officials keep the entire bribe for themselves) spreads becasue observance of law does not survive in a competitive environment" (p. 604).

Most payoffs associated with bureaucratic corruption take the form of bribery. Two consequences of bribery are generally recognized. The first, and the obvious, consequence of bribery is the redistribution of income. The second consequence of bribery has to do with its influence on performance - it is believed that bribery is sometimes helpful in improving the efficiency of bureaucracies.

Redistribution of income due to bribery will have consequences for future allocation of resources since it is possible that bribe-giver and bribe-taker allocate their marginal income differently between savings and consumption on the one hand, and between different consumption goods on the other. It is possible that the consumption versus savings behavior of receivers and givers of bribes may be different. Different consumption behavior may be due to different income levels of these two- as is well recognized in economics, as well as due to possibility that allocation of income is partly dependent upon the source of income - a concept with which economist have problems. Anthropologists, unlike economists however, have long recognized that an income of one dollar from one sources - say a legitimate one - may not be equal to an equal income from a different source - say an illegitimate one. It is possible that conversion of one "honest" dollar into one "corrupt" dollar through corruption changes the manner in which the dollar is spent. Studies by anthropologists confirm that source of income is an important determinant of consumption pattern - contradicting economists' notion that one dollar is as good as any other dollar.[22] Very little economic research is available to answer these questions. Most claims tend to be anecdotal.

Bribery is sometimes seen as bringing about improvement of performance of the bureaucrats or to increase employment.[23] Superiors of minor bureaucrats who accept bribes would see two advantages in allowing bribery to exist. "First, if the level of bribery receipts depends upon how fast low-level officials work, then corrupt bureaucrats may serve more people per day than their honest counterparts. Corruption, in this case may actually increase the efficiency of the bureaucracy. Second, the promise of corrupt gains may lower the salaries which the government must pay to attract job applicants" (Rose-Ackerman, 1978: 61).[24] In most cases, however, even those who propose this view recognize that there are many more situations where bribes lead to economically perverse behavior (Rose-Ackerman, 1978: 62-67). Tullock points out that unless markets are efficient, positions may be sold for less than what they are worth, or may be sold to people who fail to collect all the rent (1980: 23). Kurer (1993) shows how this argument falls apart if it is accepted that corruption may have been introduced deliberately by the policy makers. Kaufmann (1997) provides convincing arguments and examples to refute the fallacy that "bribery is helpful for development".

Most common argument for allowing corruption is that it "greases the wheels" of bureaucracies. Proponents of this argument ignore the discretion that politicians and bureaucrats have "over the creation, proliferation, and interpretation of counterproductive regulations" (Kaufmann 1997: 116). Possibilities of bribes are likely to motivate more burdensome regulations than less.[25] Another argument in this vein is that bribery allows the most efficient firms to operate. The theoretical basis for this argument is that most efficient firms can afford the highest bribes and hence will obtain the contacts. Kaufmann demonstrates that the argument falls apart if the low cost results from, for example, lower quality than from higher efficiency. Firms who compete for contracts when bribery is possible may bribe not only to win the contract but also to ensure that the requirements of the contract are not enforced. A weak argument for allowing corruption is cultural one: Western concepts of corruption are supposedly not applicable to emerging societies where greater reliance has to be placed on social, familial, and personal ties. There is, however, growing evidence that corruption hurts all developments efforts, not just in the industrialized countries (Kaufmann 1997: 116).

Shleifer and Vishny (1993) show that bribes have worse consequences than taxes in general equilibrium. They find that from the point of view of efficiency, competition is the best, joint monopoly is the second best, and independent monopoly is the worst (1993: 608). Kaufman (1997) provides some evidence for this.

Long term consequences of administrative corruption, though hard to quantify, may be far worse than the short term effects. It is likely that one effect of corruption is that it slowly legitimizes itself (Tanzi 1994). Moreover, the potential for a rent-seeking behavior by others (those with power to demand rent) decreases incentives for investing in innovations since rent-seeking increases uncertainty for innovative efforts. Innovators (i) are not organized into lobbies whereas existing producers are, (ii) are subject to future expropriations since their projects are long term, and (iii) face asymmetrical returns with chances of high returns being expropriated by government and bureaucrats (Murphy, Shleifer, Vishny, 1991 and 1993). Furthermore, rent-seeking competes with productive and innovative activities and if the best talent is directed to rent-seeking then economic growth is affected (Murphy, Shleifer, Vishny, 1991). Contribution of investors is reduced by a change in relative factor prices: cost of entrepreneurship increases with increase in corruption.

WHY DOES CORRUPTION PERSIST?

Why does corruption continue to exist? Why do the formal and informal checks and balances within the system not work? Where are the imperfections in the system? Corruption affects some people negatively - why are these people not able to influence the process such that corruption stops - or at least does not manifest itself in its most harmful forms? Despite the importance of these questions, very little direct attention has been devoted to them. This section of this chapter will breifly review some of the literature on political economoy of the regulatory process which seems to be the main arena in which economists have examined the imperfections in the process of economic policy formulation.

It is easiest to explain the failure of the principal-agent relationship. The principal should not normally allow its agent to make such agreements as are not in its interest. The principal, however, may not always be very effective. Besides the problem of information asymmetry which is the basis for most of the analysis of the agency issues in economics, the principal in some cases may not have full control over the agent. Agents with control over the political system can circumvent many of the checks and controls that are placed by the principal (Rose-Ackerman, 1978: 4, Etzioni-Halevy 1979, North 1984: 34, Jain 1987). The principal may, thus, lack ability to enforce the contract that it has with the agent.

In addition to the principal, competitors of the organization that plans to collude with the agent should be able to reduce the impact of collusion in a well functioning market. If different organizations can bid for the right to the monopoly rents associated with regulation, the case of collusion should be reduced to the case of directly unproductive profit-seeking activities. Given the illegal nature of the collusion in the case of corruption, however, the agent will not be able to invite public bids for purchase of the rents associated with its regulatory powers. This type of collusion will require informal channles of communication between the agent and the organization - perhaps even cultural and familial ties.[26] The market for this type of collusion may not develop because this activity requires suppression of information rather than its dissemination (Shleifer and Vishny, 1993: 611-15.)

Shleifer and Vishny (1993: 601-9) discuss other conditions that allow corruption to persist. Corruption persists because the bosses share in the spoils of the corruption process when an official sells government property for personal gains. Corruption spreads because of competition both between officials and between consumers. If the jobs are auctioned - honest officials cannot survive. Competition between officials will assure that maximal bribes are collected.[27] Furthermore, "... even more important for the spread of corruption is competition between buyers in the case with theft." (p. 604). When one consumer avoids paying full cost of goods, again the honest one will not survive. It may also be possible to draw some comparisons between enforcement of monopoly in the area of industrial organization and spread of corruption. They both require effective policing if they have to be prevented. Small numbers of those who participate in these activities lead to monopolies as well as corruption. Both these activities thrive when members of the cartel are able to punish those who break the rules of the cartel. Finally, both survive in an environment marked by secrecy (ibid).

Krueger (1993) has examined the role of political regimes in design of economic policies in developing economies. Although her objective may have been to examine why inappropriate policies persist, her analysis may form the basis for a study of persistence of corruption. Some countries "created an economic environment so inimical to growth as to cause wonderment as to why economic decline was not more precipitous" (p. 13). She finds "similarities in the policy stances across policies in those countries where economic performance has been poor" (p. 13). It is possible to speculate that the economic policies that seem so undesirable may be motivated by the self interests of those in power - who, furthermore, possess means to prevent contrary interests or control mechanisms to develop.

Clearly much work needs to be done to explain why corruption seems to get worse if it is not checked and why it seems so difficult to introduce corrective mechanisms.

ACKNOWLEDGEMENTS

The author is grateful to the Social Sciences and Humanities Research Council, Ottawa, for a grant that made this research possible.

NOTES

[1] See, among many other, Leys (1970).

[2] See Scott (1970), Wade (1985), Tanzi (1995).

[3] For the moment, we set aside the question of how the principal appoints the agent. To avoid unnecessary digression into issues surrounding the conflict between the executive and the legislative branches of the government, we assume either that they are one and the same person or that they have arranged their relationship such that they act in unison.

[4] This assumption forms the basis the agency theory. See Jensen and Meckling, (1976). See Grossman and Helpman (1994) for a model of behavior of politicians based on this assumption. We will return to this assumption below to show that there is wide spread support for the idea that the politicians look after their own interests, rather than those of the populace.

[5] The first of these relationship is used to explain corruption by, among many others, Rose-Ackerman, (1978) and Klitgaard, (1988), Shleifer and Vishny, (1992). The second relationship is emphasized by, among many others, Rose-Ackerman (1978), Shleifer and Vishny, (1992 & 1993), Tanzi, (1995). See Rose-Ackerman (1978), chapters 2-4, for an analysis of legislative corruption.

[6] See Demsetz (1984) for some elaboration.

[7] See Grossman and Helpman (1994) for modelling of purchase of politicians to influence trade policies.

[8] These activities may "...yield pecuniary returns but produce no goods or services that enter a conventional utility function directly or indirectly" (ibid) and, hence, may be seen as representing a net loss for the economy. The activities are, of course, profitable for the individual who engages in them. The conclusion that rent seeking results in waste can be criticized as being static and valid only in a system that does not consider it legitimate for

economic agents to influence government policy (Samuels and Mercuro, 1984).

[9] See Lenway, Morck, and Yeung (1996) for a recent study on the consequences of rent seeking activities.

[10] Government's ability to control, for example, foreign currency transactions - in which it controls merely the conversion between domestic and foreign currinces - results in significant rents (Krueger 1974.)

[11] Tanzi and Dawoodi (1997) provide evidence that higher corruption leads to larger expenditures on government projects which provide conduits for illegal income for decision makers.

[12] The relationship between the agent A_0 and the other agents appointed by A_0 has often been described in details. See for example, Rose-Ackerman (1978: 6-10).

[13] For one model of how the agent can do this, see Rose-Ackerman (1978: 67-74).

[14] The distinction between political and administrative corruption, however, is not very clear. See for example Wade (1985: 484).

[15] Tanzi (1995: 8-11) defines corruption in a similar manner and discusses some difficulties with such a definition.

[16] For a more detailed summary of the differences between the treatment of rent seeking in classical and neo-classical economics, see Colander (1984: 1-13).

[17] Papers in Buchanan, Tollison, and Tullock (1980) deal with various aspects of rent seeking activities.

[18] Samuels and Mercuro (1984) criticize this interpretation of rent seeking activities. The focus of those who make this interpretation would appear to be on activities like lobbying and purchase of politicians - activities which clearly only redistribute wealth.

[19] Zhou (1995) distinguishes between the behavior of insiders - who have established political links and compete with each other in a political game - and outsider - who are trying to enter an industry who compete with the insiders in an economic game. The author also distinguishes between positive sum rent seeking and negative sum rent seeking.

[20] Shleifer and Vishny (1994) describe the problems associated with "totalitarian socialism"; Kaufmann (1997) describes the problems of politicians in all types of economies making self serving decisions. All see the endnote 1 for other examples.

[21] A related, and a very important, question would be why the principals allow these agents to operate. We, however, do not address that question here.

[22] See the study by Zeliger (1994) for a thorough discussion of the what money means to people. The clearest example of the this point in that study is where the author finds that people do not use money earned through (even semi) illegitimate means, for example gambling, for donation to church. For a recent study on the impact of people's values on

their expenditure behavior, see Jain and Joy (1997). Also see work by Belk and Wellendorf (1990). Dixit, Grossman, and Helpman (1997) present a model of general agency which takes into account the non-linear nature of preferences for monetary transfers.

[23] See Ward (1989) for the later argument. We believe, however, that to be a problem associated with black market - response sometimes to poor policies. Hence, Kaufmann's (1997) refutation of "corruption is good" arguments will apply to this issue also.

[24] This view was first formalized by Leff (1964).

[25] Shleifer and Vishny refer to De Soto to state that "An important reason why many of these permits and regulations exist is probably to give officials the power to deny them and to collect bribes in return for providing the permits" (1993: 601).

[26] Tanzi (1995) explores the importance of these ties for the existence of corruption.

[27] For a proof, see Wade (1985).

REFERENCES

Barro, Robert J. (1973). "The Control of Politicians: An Economic Model," *Public Choice*, 14: 19-42.

Becker, Gary S. (1983). "A theory of competition among pressure groups for political influence," *The Quarterly Journal Of Economics*, 98 (3): 371-400.

Belk, R. W., and M. Wallendorf. (1990). "The Sacred Meaning of Money," *Journal of Economic Psychology*, 11: 35-67.

Bhagwati, Jagdish N. (1982). "Directly Unproductive, Profit-Seeking (DUP) Activities." *Journal Of Political Economy*, 90: 988-1002.

Bhagwati, Jagdish N., Richard A. Brecher and T. N. Srinivasan. (1984). "DUP Activities and Eocnomic Theory," in David C. Colander, (ed.), *Neoclassical Political Economy: The Analysis of Rent-seeking and DUP Activities*, Mass.: Ballinger Publishing Co., 17-32.

Brasz, H. A. (1970). "The Sociology of Corruption," in Arnold J. Heidenheimer, (ed.) *Political Corruption: Readings In Comparative Analysis*, New York: Holt Reinehart, 41-45.

Buchanan, James M. (1980). "Rent Seeking and Profit Seeking," in James M. Buchanan, Robert D. Tollison, and Gordon Tullock, (eds.), *Toward A Theory Of The Rent-Seeking Society*, Texas A & M University Press.

Colander, David C., (ed.) (1984). *Neoclassical Political Economy: The Analysis of Rent-seeking and DUP Activities*, Mass.: Ballinger publishing Co.

Demsetz, Harold. (1984). "Purchasing Monopoly," in David C. Colander, (ed.), *Neoclassical Political Economy: The Analysis of Rent-seeking and DUP Activities*, Mass.: Ballinger Publishing Co., 101-114.

Dixit, Avinash, Gene M. Grossman, and Elhanan Helpman,. (1997). "Common agency and Coordination: General thery and application to government policy making," *Journal of Political Economy*, 105 (4): 752-69.

Etzioni-Halevy, Eva. (1979). *Political Manipulation and Administrative Power: A Comparative Study*, International Library of Sociology, London: Routledge and Kegan Paul.

Faith, Roger L. (1980). "Rent-Seeking Aspects of Bureaucratic Competition," in James M. Buchanan, Robert D. Tollison, and Gordon Tullock, (eds.), *Toward A Theory Of The Rent-Seeking Society*, Texas A & M University Press, 332-358.

Grossman Gene M., and Elhanan Helpman. (1994). "Protection for Sale," *American Economic Review*, 84 (4): 833-50.

Heidenheimer, Arnold J. (ed.) (1970). *Political Corruption: Readings In Comparative Analysis*, New York: Holt Reinehart.

Jain, Arvind K. (1987). "Agency Problem and the International Debt Crisis." Proceedings of the Fourth Symposium on Money, Banking, and Insurance (Geld, Banken und Versicherungen), Karlsruhe, West Germany, Band I: 367-91.

_____. (1988). "An Agency Theoretic Explanation of Capital Flight." *Economics Letters*, Vol. 28, no. 1, 1988, 41-5.

_____. (1993). "Dictatorships, Democracies, and Debt Crisis." In S. P. Riley, (ed.), *The Politics Of Global Debt*, New York: St. Martin's Press.

Jain Arvind K., and Annamma Joy. (1997). "Money Matters: An Exploratory Study of the Socio-Cultural Context of Consumption, Saving, and Investment Patterns," *Journal Of Economic Psychology*, 18: 649-75.

Jensen, Michael C. and William H. Meckling. (1976). "Theory of the Firm: Managerial Behavior, Agency Costs and Ownership Structure," *The Journal of Financial Economics*, 3 (6): 305-60.

Johnston, Michael. (1982). *Political Corruption and public policy in America*, Monterey: Brooks Cole publishing. co.

Katz, Eliamim and Jacob Rosenberg. (1994). "Rent-seeking for Budgetary Allocation: Preliminary Results for 20 Countries," *Public Choice*, 60: 133-44.

Kaufmann, D. (1997). "Economic Corruption: Some Facts." Paper presented at the 8th International Anti–Corruption Conference in Lima, Perú, September.

Klitgaard, Robert. (1988). *Controlling Corruption*, Berkeley: University of California Press.

_____. (1990). *Tropical Gangsters*, New York: Basic Books.

_____. (1991). *Adjusting To Reality*, California: International Center for Economic Growth.

Krueger, Anne Osborne. (1974). "The Political Economy of the Rent-Seeking Society," *American Economic Review*, 64: 291-303.

_____. (1993). *Political Economy Of Policy Reform In Developing Countries*, Mass: MIT press.

Kurer, Oskar. (1993). "Clientelism, Corruption, and the Allocation of Resources," *Public Choice*, 77(2): 259-273.

Leff, Nathaniel H. (1964). "Economic development through bureaucratic corruption," in Arnold J. Heidenheimer, (ed.) *Political Corruption: Readings In Comparative Analysis*, New York: Holt Reinehart, 8-14.

Leiken, Robert S. (1997). "Controlling the Global Corruption Epidemic," *Foreign Policy*, no. 105: 55-76.

Lenway, Stefanie, Randall Morck, and Bernard Yeung. (1996). "Rent Seeking, Protectionism and Innovation in the American Steel Industry," *The Economic Journal*, 106: 410-421.

Leys, Colin. (1970). "What is the problem about corruption?" in Arnold J. Heidenheimer, (ed.) *Political Corruption: Readings In Comparative Analysis*, New York: Holt Reinehart, 31- 37.

Lien, Da-Hsiang Donald. (1990). "Corruption and allocation efficiency," *Journal of Development Economics*, 33: 153-64.

Mauro, Paolo. (1995). "Corruption and Growth," *Quarterly Journal of Economics*, 110(3): 681-712.

Mixon, F. G., Jr., D. N. Laband and R. B. Ekelund Jr. (1994). "Rent seeking and hidden in-kind resource distortion: Some empirical evidence," *Public Choice*, 78(2): 171-186.

Murphy, Kevin, M., Andrei Shleifer and Robert Vishny. (1991). "The Allocation of Talent: Implications for Growth." *Quarterly Journal Of Economics*, 106: 503-30.

_____. (1993). "Why is Rent-Seeking so Costly to Growth?" *American Economic Review*, 82(2): 409-414.

North, Douglas. (1984). "Three Approaches to the Study of Institutions," in David C. Colander, (ed.), *Neoclassical Political Economy: The Analysis of Rent-seeking and DUP Activities*, Mass.: Ballinger publishing Co., 33-40.

Paul, Chris, and Al Wilhite. (1994). "Illegal markets and the social costs of rent-seeking," *Public Choice*, Vol. 79 (1-2): 105-116.

Rose-Ackerman, Susan. (1978). *Corruption: A Study in Political Economy*. Academic Press.

Samuels, Warren J., and Nicholas Mercuro. (1984). "A Critique of Rent-Seeking Theory," in David C. Colander, (ed.), *Neoclassical Political Economy: The Analysis of Rent-seeking and DUP Activities*, Mass.: Ballinger publishing Co., 55-70.

Scott, James C. (1970). "Corruption, Machine Politics, and Political Change," in Arnold J. Heidenheimer, (ed.) *Political Corruption: Readings In Comparative Analysis*, New York: Holt Reinehart, 549-563.

Shleifer, Andrei and Robert Vishny. (1992). "Pervasive Shortages Under Socialism," *RAND Journal of Economics*, 23(2): 237-246.

_____. (1993). "Corruption." *Quarterly Journal of Economics*, 108(3): 99-617.

_____. (1994). "The politics of market socialism," *Journal of Economic Perspectives*, 8 (2): 165-176.

Tanzi, Vito, 1995, "Corruption, Government Activities, and Markets." In Gianluca Fiorentini and Sam Petzman (eds.), *The Economics of Organized Crime*, Cambridge: Cambridge University Press.

Tanzi, V. and Davoodi, H. (1997). "Corruption, Public Investment, and Growth." IMF Working Paper WP/97/139.

Tullock, Gordon. (1980). "Rent Seeking as a Negative-Sum Game," in James M. Buchanan, Robert D. Tollison, and Gordon Tullock, (eds.), *Toward A Theory Of The Rent-Seeking Society*, Texas A & M University Press, 16-36.

_____. (1993). *Rent Seeking*, The Shaftesbury papers, 2, U.K.: Hants Edward Elgar.

Wade, Robert. (1985). "The market for public office: Why the Indian state is not better at development" *World Development*, 13 (4): 467-97.

Ward, Peter M. (1989). *Corruption, Development And Inequality*, London: Routledge.

Zhou, H. (1995). "Rent seeking and market competition," *Public Choice*, 82 (3-4): 225-241.

3

CORRUPTION IN THE MODERN ARMS BUSINESS: *LESSONS FROM THE PENTAGON SCANDALS*[1]

R. T. NAYLOR
McGill University

For all the difficulties that exist in arriving at a widely acceptable definition of "corruption", there is little doubt that it can play an insidious role in debasing political morality, undermining public institutions and wasting collective resources, particularly tax revenues. However, "corruption" involves much more than simply long-suffering transnational corporations having to meet the extra cost of doing business "in that part of the world", as those on the paying side so often claim in self-defense. It involves much more than simply vulnerable countries having their underpaid public servants suborned by greedy transnational corporations, as those on the receiving end so often insist in self-justification. Therefore the response lies not just in passing laws whose only result will be to drive the phenomenon further underground where it will be even more difficult to detect and eradicate. Prior to any broad-based attack on systemic "corruption", it is essential to understand its historical roots, the precise role it plays in corporate and political cultures, and the way a prevailing ideology may serve as a rationalization for its continued existence.

Nowhere are the depth and strength of these roots, and the complexity of the corporate and political matrix in which they are fixed, better illustrated than in the arms business. For more than a century across the entire globe, the weapons business has been a dirty business.[2] Nor can this be imputed to simply an elemental crudeness often typical of emergent capitalism in countries without a well-developed commercial or regulatory infrastructure. For one of the most notorious yet representative instances has been the Pentagon scandals of the 1980s. As they so well demonstrate, arms are produced and traded in a system in which hypocrisy and deception are the norm and in which waste of public resources is the very *raison d'être*. As a result, "corruption" became endemic in virtually every possible form - fraudulent cost inflation, bribery, influence peddling, industrial espionage, trading with embargoed locations and laundering payment flows.

Yet it could be argued that such acts of criminality are not the real problem, and that focusing on "corruption" *per se* may steer public debate onto a distinctly second-order issue. It is possible that the main subject of concern should be not why this or that item procured by the military costs so much, or how this or that weapon ended up in some unauthorized destination. Rather it should be how so much of society's productive potential became - and remains - captive of an industrial complex that is dedicated to the production of something which is, at best, useless from the point of view of promoting human economic well-being, and, at worst, extremely detrimental.

Arguably this greater corruption at the societal level, the product of colluding corporations, opportunistic politicians and a military establishment intent on self-perpetuation, dwarfs the payoffs and kickbacks, padded invoices and phony end-user certificates, that are merely the daily (and likely essential) operational methods of the arms business. Without understanding and addressing that larger context - its origins, nature and modus operandi - anti-corruption measures (much like anti-drug initiatives) will merely succeed in changing the methods by which corruption occurs and/or shifting the immediate identity of the corrupter while leaving the systemic problem largely intact.

THE CULTURE OF CORRUPTION TAKES ROOT

In classical times the arms industry was run directly by the state, both to assure a continuous supply to its own forces and to inhibit weaponry from getting into the hands of the enemy. An independent and entrepreneurial arms industry emerged in Europe first in the city of Liège, in what is now Belgium, in the 14th century. Almost from its inception it showed a propensity to seek customers wherever it could find them. When Charles the Bald, Duke of Burgundy, issued an edict ordering the city to desist, and the city defied him, he burned it down and killed every inhabitant he could find. This rather radical attempt at a supply-side solution did little good. The city was quickly rebuilt and business was soon flourishing again (Thayer 1969: 22).

However, while restrictions on the choice of customer were routinely flaunted - in Elizabethan England the estimate was that 80% of all cannons manufactured were smuggled abroad - there was little opportunity for dishonest methods on the production side. Until the nineteenth century the arms industry was mainly organized as small-scale workshops run by master-craftsmen who would fabricate an entire weapon from start to finish, using traditional methods and following traditional models. On occasion gifted dilettantes would turn their talents to military design - Leonardo da Vinci, for example, may have taken as much pride in drafting plans for the world's first breech-loading cannon as he did in creating the *Mona Lisa* (Howe 1980: 317). But not until well into the 19th century was there any science devoted specifically to military production. Moreover, until then armies consisted of a small core of professionals around which rag-tag collections of amateurs would be forcibly inducted when the need arose. Therefore they had little use for anything besides the tried-and-true basics. With the exception of cannons, cast mainly in state-owned factories, the great bulk of an army's needs could be met by civilian industries to whom the state appeared as merely one customer among many - and probably slower than most to pay the bills.

Transformation of the business into its modern form came in three distinct stages. First was the combined impact of Napoleon and the Industrial Revolution. Napoleon's "citizen-army", based on the mass mobilization of ideologically-motivated freemen, became the model for the professional organizations that followed. Meanwhile the progress of industrialization permitted the new, large-scale armies to equip each soldier with the same type of weapon, built to use identical ammunition and constructed of interchangeable parts. Mass armies meant mass orders, and therefore required to meet them, large-scale businesses for whom the stakes in serving the demands of the state were potentially enormous. By the middle of the 19th century major arms makers were at work in Britain, France, Prussia, Russia, Japan and especially in the US. There, during the Civil War, military demands for the first time took precedence over the needs of the civilian economy; the government subsidized large-scale factory production of arms by the private sector; and, not least, the war brought to the fore the standards of commercial morality that would subsequently typify so many military suppliers.

Contractors bribed officials into accepting shoddy clothing, faulty tents and blankets, and adulterated food. When wartime disturbances to trade and increased danger from privateers reduced international and coastal commerce, ship-owners with idle vessels connived to sell them to the government. They were aided and abetted by the government's own purchasing agents who would accept payoffs from owners seeking to unload the most antiquated and dangerous vessels in their fleets - that was one of the foundations of the Vanderbilt fortune, for example. The same standards held true in the provision of weapons. While his father, a powerful merchant banker, was arranging for the sale of US government war bonds in England, a young J. P. Morgan was dividing his energies between avoiding the draft and plotting to have the US government float part of the proceeds of those bond sales into his bank accounts. His first independent business transaction took place when the federal government sold off a batch of obsolete and defective carbines. Working through a front-man, Morgan bought them for $3.50 each, then talked a Union general into buying them, supposedly new and in perfect condition, for $22.00 a piece. When soldiers using the first shipment began blowing their thumbs off, the government canceled the order and refused to pay, at which point Morgan successfully sued for recovery of most of what was owing.[3]

At this stage military contracting was a quick path to riches, but not one which the beneficiaries could seek to exploit on a long term basis. After the war, the business elite shifted its attention back to civilian activities - plundering the public purse through railroad jobs was far more lucrative than selling mouldy grain in underweight sacks to a rapidly shrinking army. Still, they did not neglect the occasional chance to work their "captains of industry" magic on weapons contracts. In 1893 Andrew Carnegie, the steel tycoon, was charged by the US Secretary of the Navy with conspiring to hide critical flaws in armor plate.

Carnegie's brief, and ultimately costless brush with the authorities over a naval contract, signaled the second stage in the emergence of a modern weapons industry. For hundreds of years the main difference between a merchant vessel, which was always armed, and a naval ship was more a matter of who paid the sailors than on what they sailed. But towards the end of the 19th century, a new global arms race began, centered around enormous armor-plated warships. Unlike the mass production of small arms and ammunition, which could be done by firms capable of shifting back again to civilian production with little difficulty, the new warships required a long lead time for specialized design, the investment of large sums of money up front to cover overhead costs and a huge financial commitment to purchase the specialized inputs necessary to make a very few units of technologically-sophisticated output. The loss of the revenues from the sale of even a single one of those products could spell financial disaster. The result was a subtle but important transformation of the connection of the supplier to the customer. Instead of an arms-length relationship, sometimes solidified by bribery for particular deals, the two sides would be welded together as surely as the steel plates on a *dreadnought*'s hull (Kaufman 1970: xx-xxi).

Not coincidentally it was in the production and sale of warships that the 20th century's first great arms scandals occurred. In 1909 Britain's Coventry Ordnance secured orders to build eight cruisers by publishing false figures about the size of the German fleet. In 1913 Germany's Alfred Krupp was caught paying naval officers for information on secret government projects. The next year Britain's Vickers found itself in the spotlight over an attempt to bribe Japanese officials to win a battleship contract from a rival. In a remarkable portent of the notorious 1970s scandal involving the sale of Lockheed jets to Japan, the battleship affair culminated in the jailing of a Japanese rear admiral who had toured British arms producers collecting kickbacks, and in the forced resignation of the Japanese prime minister.[4]

It was such an environment that produced Sir Basil Zaharoff, a pioneer of methods which would subsequently become standard procedures in his chosen craft. Born, appropriately enough, in the most notorious red-light district of Istanbul, Zaharoff began business as a brothel tout before learning the arts of black market money exchange and loan sharking. In a remarkable portent of his career as an arms salesmen, he may also have been a member of the fire-brigade in a quarter where the firemen were notorious for setting blazes and then extorting bribes to put them out. Subsequently in London, Zaharoff cheated a business associate of £7,000, then ran off to Cyprus with the money to start a new career selling weapons. After one abortive scheme in which he and a confederate unsuccessfully tried to steal military plans and equipment off an Austrian warship - his partner was killed in the attempt - Zaharoff got his big break. At a time when the political temperature in the Balkans was reaching the boiling point, he secured the job of local representative of the Swedish Nordenfelt firm by lying about his supposed connections to British intelligence.

In the course of his successful career, Zaharoff bribed purchasing officials and lavishly entertained politicians and senior military officers, particularly in brothels and casinos where he sometimes held a financial interest. He made a point of selling to one side, rushing off to tell the other side what their enemy had acquired, then, after securing offsetting orders, returning to the first side to sell even more. He learned how to play on local ethno-sectarian tensions, for example by impressing on Greek politicians the need to rearm in order to "win back Asian minor". He would sabotage rival products or claim their proven accomplishments for his own merchandise. And he was among the first, if not the first, to realize the importance of arranging financing for his customers, persuading banks and financial houses to lend money for arms purchases, something they always avoided in the past. Not least, during the first world war, while weighing in heavily on the side of Britain and France, he ensured that his factories in central Europe fulfilled their contractual requirements to the other side.[5]

Despite the pre-war fever for huge warships, during the actual conflict the heaviest expenditures were actually land-based, for equipping and maintaining infantry, for the means of transporting troops and supplies, and for the high explosives gulped down by great parks of artillery. And after the war, most industries found it easy to make the transition to the civilian market with its prodigious appetite for canned and preserved foods, synthetic textiles, automobiles, electrical products, and industrial and agricultural chemicals. Du Pont, for example, whose rise through the industrial and political ranks had begun with its control of most of the gunpowder supplies during the American Civil War, managed to collect enough war booty from this latest conflict in the form of German patents for synthetic chemical processes that it never again had to rely on the military sector for its prosperity.

But even though most industrialists moved back to civilian activities, their previous unprecedented involvement in the war effort left a permanent impact on the principles - financial and commercial - that would later guide the business relations of weapons producers and the government. During the war the industry had not only had free access to the public purse, but felt little obligation to contribute to it. Both the British and American governments, facing demands by organized labor for the conscription of wealth as well as manpower, would periodically decry profiteering and prosecute the occasional contractor whose methods proved excessively crude, while permitting the weapons makers to defer declaring their profits until after the war when the corporate tax rates were slashed.[6] Furthermore, during the war, the principle was established that such a national emergency justified handing out military contracts without any semblance of competitive bidding. And in the aftermath of the war, yet more precedents were set.

For those firms who remained in the arms business, the next two decades were difficult. Government orders shrunk, and the competition for what remained was vociferous. Skillful marketing therefore took on a new significance. It was no longer a matter of manufacturers or their agents convincing governments that their products suited military requirements better than those of their competitors. Rather it was a matter of convincing governments they needed any product at all, regardless of who produced it. The role of bribery accordingly shifted from helping the buyer decide between alternative sources of supply to convincing government purchasing officials of the "national security" urgency of whatever the arms dealer had to offer (Sampson 1977: 54-5). In a harbinger of what would occur on a massive scale during the Cold War era, in the 1930s the Romanian agent of

Czechoslovakia's Skoda works, which alone accounted for nearly 10% of all world arms sales, was caught not only evading taxes, bribing officials and engaging in industrial espionage, but also fabricating evidence of a planned Soviet invasion.

Excusing the Inexcusable

However, these antics also increased the moral vulnerability of the industry at an awkward juncture in its history. Outside the closed rooms where the deals were hatched was a population traumatized by the unprecedented slaughter they had just witnessed.[7] The public at large desperately sought to exorcise the demon of war; while the politicians responsible for the carnage looked for a way of deflecting the heat. The arms manufacturers and their salesmen were a target that was not merely obvious, but remarkably easy, given their record of payoffs, extortion, bid-rigging, shoddy manufacturing, sabotage of competing products, and trading with the enemy. Thus the notion became widely accepted that war was caused, not by commercial greed, political ambition or military brinkmanship, but by the conniving of the "merchants of death" (Howe 1980: 327).

Of course, the movers and makers of the arms industry had their rebuttals ready. No less a figure that Sir Basil Zaharoff insisted to the British authorities that his network of agents in pre-war Germany had been not just peddling weapons, but also creating an intelligence organization able to tip off the Allies about German military intentions - carefully sidestepping the fact that those intentions might have been considerably less dangerous had his agents not been doing their official job so well. Similarly, firms caught selling to their own countries' potential enemies would point to all the money they were bringing home and how many jobs the foreign sales supported (Kaufman 1970: 18). These types of arguments - that arms sales served an intelligence function, and that they were essentially to a country's economic and financial health - would come to figure prominently in the rhetoric of arms makers in future decades whenever they were caught in the act of pushing their products in legally or morally unacceptable locations.

Apart for the need for a scapegoat after the first world war, there were several reasons why the industry was so vulnerable, both to huge fluctuations in the demand for its product and to the vagaries of public opinion. Wars were episodic and enemies came and went. And resources committed to the military were seen as lost to the civilian economy, something that could only be acceptable in times of national emergency. Ivory tower economists of the early 20th century expounded enthusiastically before wide-eyed students about the conflict between a society's capacity to manufacture guns and its ability to produce butter. This "trade-off curve" could be found proudly entrenched in the opening chapters of virtually every introductory college economics textbook. All of this fed a general peacetime revulsion against the arms industry and led to efforts to bring it under severe government regulation or to nationalize it outright.

When the second World War broke out, the arms makers won a reprieve. They could once again pose as the corporate citizens of the hour. Still, the expectation was that peace would bring the usual reaction, moral and material. This time, however, the expectation was wrong. A little miracle happened. The enemy did not go away. Preparation for war became a permanent phenomenon. And the war industry itself came to be viewed, not as a cost imposed on the civilian economy, reducing living standards, but as just the opposite. The third and last stage in the evolution of a modern arms industry had begun.

The new doctrine about the positive economic effects of military expenditure drew its inspiration from two sources. One was a misinterpretation of the reasons why Germany had escaped the Great Depression ahead of the rest of Europe. Although the actual driving force was the success of the Nazi public works program, especially road-building (Overy 1994: 5-9), a more convenient explanation, which also helped rationalize early French and British military reverses, was that Germany rose to prosperity on the crest of a rearmament wave.

The second were the canons of Keynesian economics and the role they postulated for deficit spending. Neatly twisted from a short-term prescription for pump-priming economies caught in the trough of a business cycle into a long-term theory of contra-cyclical demand management, it was simple enough to take the dogma one step further. Government expenditures on domestically produced weapons came to be regarded as a tool for accomplishing three distinct goals - smoothing out cyclical ups and downs in general business conditions, assuring the stability of employment and the growth of national income over the long run, and, as a bonus, guaranteeing that countries could stay at the forefront of technological innovation through reaping the spillovers from investment in military research and development.

In reality military expenditures have always made a poor economic stabilizer. Large projects require a long lead time, and they cannot be easily scheduled to start just when the economy is in a down phase. Furthermore, once the commitment is made to a big expenditure flow, it is difficult or impossible to turn it off, so that the peak of the spending may come after the economy has already started to heat up. The number of jobs typically produced is much less than by the equivalent spending on civilian projects;

and they are almost always created for people with the kinds of skills that easily find employment elsewhere (Nincic 1982: 50). Even the technological benefits are exaggerated. While the American military pioneered much of the modern aerospace, communications, and electronics technology, not only could the civilian sector have probably done it just as well, or better (as the Japanese experience showed) if it had had the same amount of government support, but, in more recent years, the military has borrowed from the civilian sector as much or more than the other way around.[8]

Nonetheless, military spending as a tool of government economic policy had this striking advantage - no one could question it on ideological grounds. Everyone is automatically in favor of "national security". And business interests, which would viscerally oppose increases in expenditure on health, education and welfare, the obvious alternative means by which the government could stimulate the economy, were generally delighted with the decision to lavish on a core part of the industrial structure so much public money. Nowhere was this better appreciated than in the US where the government, haunted by the twin specters of another Great Depression at home and triumphant communism abroad, took the lead in breaking with tradition and keeping its military machine tooled up. While both specters turned out to be chimerical, they sufficed to bring the "permanent war economy" into existence, and, along with it, unprecedented opportunities for corporate fraud.

THE PERMANENT WAR CONTRACTORS' ECONOMY

In the early years, even though the overall level of military spending remained well above previous peace-time norms, in one sense it continued to follow its historical pattern. It would rise during hostilities - such as the Korean War - and fall afterwards. Furthermore, throughout the 1950s and 1960s most of the money was spent in traditional ways, equipping large forces with equipment that, while heavier, deadlier and more sophisticated than the material of the past, would not have seemed particularly space-age to a second world war veteran. In the 1970s both of those features changed. Prodded on partly by genuine excitement about new possibilities in the aerospace, communications and electronics fields, and partly by the backlash from Vietnam with its heavy human casualties and even heavier political ones, new equipment produced for the Pentagon, the world trend-setter, became increasingly complex, stressing science over manpower, aerospace over land-based activities. And, although the overall US military budget did decline sharply following the end of the Vietnam war, for the first time in American history, the arms *procurement* part actually grew after a major conflict. With a few short-lived setbacks, it kept on growing for nearly two decades. Increasingly a core group of large corporations, with enormous overheads to cover, had a growing share of their production facilities committed to making ultra-sophisticated, high-cost items for a single customer. While in the pre-world war one era this incestuous relationship between big arms contractors and the government, with all its attendant ills and opportunities for corruption, had been limited to the shipyards, by the 1970s it pervaded virtually the entire high-tech sector of modern American industry. Furthermore, there seemed to be an indisputable rationalization for it.

The image of aggressively expansionist communism was contrived shortly after the second world war, at a time when the Soviet Union had lost 20 million people and most of its heavy industry, by an American intelligence apparatus desperate to find a continued rationale for its own existence (Knightley 1986: 248). The idea that the West, led by the US, was lagging behind the USSR in military spending subsequently became a common theme in US presidential campaigns and was hammered home with special force whenever the need arose to legitimize especially large increases. In the wake of the Korean war, Dwight Eisenhower revealed the "bomber gap". John F. Kennedy in his 1960 campaign discovered a "missile gap" at a time when the US had hundreds in service and the USSR had managed to deploy six. This campaign reached its apogee in Ronald Reagan's first State of the Union address in which, based on CIA estimates, he announced a "spending gap" over the previous decade of more than $300 billion.[9]

Making such comparative calculations involving widely different economic and political systems is always difficult. To meet the challenge, the CIA converted *ruble* figures into dollars at the official (instead of the more accurate, black market) exchange rate; it used US prices for the many thousands of items for which it could find no *ruble* value; it imputed to Soviet soldiers, some of them with rags wrapped around their feet, the same standard of living as US soldiers; it included all Soviet military spending (about one quarter of which was committed to the China theater), instead of just that involved in confronting NATO; it failed to factor out of the Soviet numbers many things like civil defense, internal security, building infrastructure in remote areas etc. that had no equivalent in the US military budget; and it made no adjustment for the fact that the USSR paid most of the costs of its Warsaw Pact allies, whereas the NATO countries were self-financing. If the actual spending figures were modified to take these factors into account, not only did the "spending gap" disappear, but the US and its allies ended up outspending the USSR and Warsaw Pact by some $700 billion over that same decade.[10]

Still, the "spending gap" did its job, rationalizing the biggest arms build-up in US peace-time history.[11] During the 1980s the Pentagon was doling out, at peak, $28 million per hour, of which about 40% (more than $100 billion per year) went to buying hardware. Not only did the overall military budget shoot up, but the "black budget", the ultra-secret portion, grew so rapidly during the Reagan years that it accounted at peak for 12% of all military spending, upwards of $36 billion per year, a sum larger than the entire military budget of any other country except the USSR. "Black" programs had one genuine purpose - such a classification helped increase security around new weapons developments. But they could also have three other, more duplicitous uses. They provided cover for funding intelligence agency covert operations; they gave certain privileged military-industrial firms a lever for extracting extra money, since no one questioned how much was being spent on supposedly top-secret, state-of-the-art weaponry; and they were excellent for covering up stupidity, waste and fraud of which there was an abundance.[12]

In such an environment, cheered on by politicians who saw in the arms business both jobs for their constituents (plants were deliberately placed in as many congressional districts as possible) and a source of electoral slush funds, and by trade unions and scientific lobbies, the military contractors got bigger and fatter. They were flush with cash even in times of recession when civilian firms were hurting; their profit rates were consistently higher than those of most large non-military firms; and their stock market performance was·better - much to the delight of investment counselors and fund managers with rate of return targets to meet. In short, a very powerful and varied set of vested interests emerged committed to protecting a weapons-supply complex in which there was no competitive bidding, and in which a whole gamut of tax breaks, subsidies, exemptions and privileges were taken for granted, including a *de facto* immunity from any really serious consequences of criminal behavior (Kaufman 1970: xv-xvi).

GAMES ARMS MANUFACTURERS PLAY

Although contractor fraud had been a matter of some concern from the start of the permanent war economy, the biggest scandals in the early years were caused by overseas sales tactics, particularly by the giant aerospace firms, rather than by domestic production methods. Although all of the major manufacturers were caught bribing foreign officials and politicians to secure sales, it was Lockheed Corporation that attracted the most unwanted attention.[13]

Two things made Lockheed's sales drive especially energetic. One was the fact that the US Department of Defense, backed by a Treasury worried about the US balance of payments, had been pushing hard since the early 1960s for standardization of NATO forces around American models - and for making sure that all allies who could afford to do so paid full cost for their material. The second was that the main item in the Lockheed catalog, the *Starfighter*, was regarded as too unreliable for the US itself to buy, putting pressure on the company to peddle all the harder abroad. In the process of hawking its wares, Lockheed had become a big contributor to everything from a fake Widows and Orphans fund of the Indonesian Air Force to the coffers of the Christian Social Union Party of Germany, then headed by the country's defense minister. In Italy, Saudi Arabia, the Netherlands - the plot was roughly the same, with small sub-variants depending on who the local agents were.

Lockheed's choices of sales agents were certainly eclectic. In Italy it had picked a former fighter pilot for Mussolini, who was a militant of the neo-fascist MSI party and had just been implicated in an ultra-right wing coup attempt. In the Netherlands, the corporation had contributed handsomely to the entertainment expenses of an impecunious Crown Prince who had trouble reconciling his wife's parsimony with his own taste for high-profile, high-price tag love affairs. But nowhere was the choice more interesting, and perhaps more representative of the nature of the alliances necessary for success in the emerging international aerospace market than in Japan. There Lockheed relied for its success on a member of parliament who was soon convicted of embezzlement, a series of former wartime intelligence officers who had been purged by the US occupation forces, and two of Japan's most powerful gangsters. One of them was a billionaire who had made his money in the post-war gasoline black-market. The other was a former ultra-nationalist agitator who had been responsible for organizing the mass looting of raw materials in Manchuria and for trafficking in heroin throughout China during the war. Jailed after the war as a Class A War Criminal and with a possible death sentence hanging over his head, he was released as part of the new war on Communism. With his newfound respectability, he got busy funding the rise of the Liberal Democratic Party and acting as money manager for the most important *yakuza* faction, before Lockheed came calling, employing him as their chief agent of influence to launder the bribe money they were running to tie up the Japanese market.[14]

All of this went on for years without detection until a series of unfortunate accidents. A US Congressional investigation into the Watergate scandal turned up some leads pointing to illegal corporate donations to the

Nixon re-election campaign. One of the firms implicated was Lockheed's rival, Northrop Corporation. And a closer look at Northrop showed that the illegal election contributions followed the same trail as a flow of corruption money to foreign agents to secure overseas orders. When Northrop was subsequently grilled about its methods, it pleaded in its own defense that its "consultancy system" had been modeled on that of Lockheed. And when Lockheed in turn was called to account, it told its critics that since the cost of the bribes was simply added to the price of the planes, it was taxpayers in the purchasing countries, not in the US, that covered the cost - so what was the fuss all about?

Lockheed's pleas failed to impress. The scandal ultimately led to the passage of the Foreign Corrupt Practices Act, making bribery by American firms to secure foreign contracts a criminal offense. The main immediate effect of the new regulations was less to reduce corruption than to force corporations to use more sophisticated methods for laundering the cash. And the public exposure simply served to educate envious and ambitious firms elsewhere in the world about the rules of business deportment necessary to break the American position of dominance in "free world" arms sales. Nonetheless, it was precisely this statute that would set off, albeit belatedly, a world-wide debate over the need for transparency in commercial transactions in an effort to root out corruption – although arguably the driving force was and remains not morality but the need for US firms to make sure that their European and South Asian rivals have to face the same obstacles to and potential penalties for using corrupt methods, along with the general desire of cost-cutting corporations to not have to pay in bribes what they are already evading in taxes.[15]

To be sure, there were also scandals involving American military contractors' relations with the US department of defense as well. The first major one came in the 1960s when the Pentagon and Lockheed were caught jointly trying to falsify performance results and cost data to protect both the Pentagon's grossly inflated military transport-plane program and Lockheed's equally hyped stock market price. That seemed a window of opportunity for reformers to argue for the abandonment of the long-standing practice of "historical cost pricing" - the principle that the starting point for pricing each new weapon should be the final price of the previous model, no matter how severe its cost overruns might have been. In its stead they pressed for "should-cost pricing" - the rather sensible principle that estimates of an item's cost should be based on the open market price of the labor and materials necessary to make it.[16] Three decades later, historical cost pricing remains the norm. About the only thing that changed was how much taxpayers' money was available for misappropriation.[17]

During the great arms expenditure boom of the 1980s, tactics used to illegally siphon off public money went through two phases. In the early part of the decade, when the money flowed most freely, competition between arms contractors turned largely on who could squeeze the most profit from a given job. One technique was to cheat on materials - billing for full cost but cutting corners by using inferior materials, or only partially completing the job. So it was with one firm that was caught plating naval vehicles with sub-standard steel. This kind of scam might sometimes be accompanied by fake test results - the kind that secured Northrop Corporation another criminal charge, this time for false claims regarding the performance of its naval aircraft and air force cruise missiles.

The real action, though, lay not in scrimping on materials but in puffing the costs. That, in turn, could take two distinct forms. One was to load onto the Department of Defense the cost of totally bogus items - hair cuts, golf course fees, baby sitters' wages, seasons' tickets to sporting events, even charges from a kennel for minding an executive's dog.[18] Some of the items seemed such penny-ante rip-offs that the only apparent explanation for such behavior by hugely wealthy corporations seemed to be that fraudulently inflating costs had become an automatic reflex. Thus, Martin Marietta arranged with a travel agency to get rebates on bulk air-fares for its officers, and then billed the Department of Defense for the full sum; while Pratt & Whitney charged to the taxpayer the cost of a Halloween party held to boost employee morale plus a $67,000 donation to an arts society favored by the wives of some Air Force generals.[19] On the other hand, some like Northrop were both more demanding and more honest – a $10 million item on the bottom of an internal cost calculation for MX missile parts read "Room for Pad". It also undertook a detailed analysis of different methods of accounting, noting that one had the advantage of being "honest" – the company then picked a different one.[20]

The second cost-puffing technique was more insidious, and harder to detect. It involved the artificial inflation of costs associated with actually performing the job. Sometimes they were labor costs that were aggressively padded.[21] More often the falsification involved component costs - the realm of the $7,622 coffee maker, $743 pliers and $640 on-board toilet seat.[22] These practices were facilitated by the fact that, by the mid 1980s, most of the major defense contractors had installed state-of-the-art computerized accounting systems which made it trivially easy to co-mingle government and commercial costs. Contractors who exceeded their cost targets on one project could shift the excess onto others that were under target, so that the government, rather than the contractor, paid the full cost of the overruns. And if a contractor had over-budgeted for wasted, damaged and lost materials and parts, the surplus could be shifted elsewhere and used for free.[23] In 1988 Sundstrand Corporation, suppliers of electrical components for aircraft, was caught over-billing by more than $125 million, then forging some records and destroying others to cover it up.[24]

Until 1986 the money flowed almost without interruption. But that year budgetary restrictions caused some cutbacks while the public backlash from cost-inflation scandals led to an announced shift towards a more competitive bidding process. In fact, both of these changes were exaggerated for public relations purposes. The cutbacks still left the military budget nearly a third above its pre-Reagan level; and the Pentagon's definition of "competition" bore a greater resemblance to a back-room confab between golf buddies than it did a cut-throat price war between rival suppliers.[25] Furthermore, to the extent that the changes had any impact, it was not in reducing the amount of defense fraud, but shifting its nature. The real action became trafficking in inside information to assure a firm either bested its rivals to secure a contract or arrived at an accommodation with them to rig the bids. And the key to a firm's success in doing either came to depend on "consultants" hired to wheel and deal, bribe and steal, on its behalf.[26]

Consultants had two major roles. The first was collecting information on behalf of client corporations about pending programs, an art that was especially important as the "black budget" increased in relative size and as big ticket items became increasingly rare.[27] To do the job, consultants had to be able to open up both bureau doors and office safes. It was a good business, all the more so since consultants were known to double-cross clients by selling the same information to competing companies.[28] They also developed a more proactive role. As more and more power within the military shifted from operations to procurement, the initiative for new weapons came increasingly from the private sector. Consultants would also pick up ideas for new arms projects from contractors and go to work inside the Pentagon, whipping up enthusiasm. Then, when the service involved drew up specifications, the consultant was on hand to advise on what to include and how to write them so as to favor a particular company he was representing. Whether operating in reactive or proactive modes, the consultants could not have done their job without inside help, help that would be rendered by defense officials for three reasons - friendship (the old boys network), the prospect of a future job or the lure of a current bribe.[29]

The military's obsession with high-tech, high-cost solutions to old problems along with the manufacturers' willingness and ability to cut costly corners combined to produce results that were sometimes comical - as in the case of an air-force anti-tank missile that consistently missed the targeted tanks but proved lethal to telephone poles. But sometimes they were tragic, rarely more so than with the Aegis, a tracking system that was supposed to permit a ship to detect multiple possible attackers, select and prioritize the threats, and prime and fire missiles virtually automatically. Built by Unisys under a contract apparently steered to them by a bribed senior official in the US Navy, the Aegis system inspired so much enthusiasm in the Navy that positive results from testing under the most favorable possible conditions were issued to the public, while those made under less favorable conditions, which were uniformly negative, were stamped "top secret" and successfully buried. The multibillion dollar system managed in its early combat experience to miss completely a plane that approached well within the range that someone equipped with a standard pair of binoculars could easily have spotted, and its proponents claimed it had managed to locate for destruction a Libyan patrol boat that turned out to be a low-flying rain cloud. But the Aegis system's moment of greatest glory came when it decided that an Iranian civilian airliner with 290 people on board was an attacking F-14 fighter - even though the civil aircraft was no more than five miles off its designated flight-path, was ascending instead of descending, and was moving 100 knots slower than an attacking F-14 would.[30]

JUSTICE FOR ALL?

When the second round of scandals broke - this time revolving around the consultancy system - the optimistic prognosis was that the Pentagon would never be the same. But once more very little actually happened and even less changed. General Electric, for example, managed in the four years after the announced "clean-up" of procurement practices to collect fully 16 new criminal charges, compared to "only" four by the next in the line-up, McDonnell-Douglas, without it affecting in the slightest its defense department career.[31]

There were many reasons for the resilience of a system based on cronyism, espionage, payoffs, accounting fraud and faked performance tests. First, the entire military-industrial complex was and remains surrounded by protective constituencies. Apart from the economic clout of the companies, there was the entrenched power of a military establishment in which the most desirable jobs had become those in procurement rather than operations. And the military were committed to protecting the major suppliers both to assure the flow of hardware and to enhance and the prospects of future corporate positions for senior officers when their turn at the revolving door rolled round. There were also unions determined to put their members' job security in arms factories ahead of any notion of proletarian solidarity with the people against whom the weapons were supposed to be used. After all, where else could people find jobs that permitted them to manufacture jewelry, make decoders to view cable TV without charge, and peddle insurance, real estate, stocks, diet foods, and cosmetics at government expense?[32] And then there were politicians who found the arms industry a source of prosperity both for their constituents and for their election coffers. Political contributions by arms contractors jumped nine fold during the salad days in the first half of the 1980s.[33]

All of those layers of protection made going after military procurement fraud a potential career minefield for investigators and prosecutors. And even if they were brave enough to try, there were many obstacles standing in the way of success.

One was the difficulty of breaking into the closed circuit of officials, consultants and industry executives. Too often investigation and prosecution had to rely on whistle-blowers. Operating under the 1863 False Claims Act passed at the request of President Lincoln to deal with Civil War profiteers (and strengthened in the early 1980s) whistle-blowers were entitled to a big cut of whatever was recovered from the companies targeted. Effective though bounty hunting may have been in other aspects of US law enforcement, very few cases of arms procurement fraud have been so exposed. Singer Corporation, caught effectively with two sets of books, was an exception, probably because revolving doors can, on rare occasions, swing both ways. A former Singer employee joined the Pentagon and then spilled the beans, prompted, he claimed, by patriotic sentiments, though the prospect of collecting 20 percent of anything Singer had to cough up certainly helped bring those sentiments into the open.[34]

Then there were all kinds of special problems involved in actually prosecuting. The relevant documents might well be classified top secret, before or after the investigation began. For those not so protected, there was the sheer mass. When prosecutors sought to prove that Bell Aerospace had cooked the books on its helicopters, and demanded documents, they were duly obliged with three tractor trailers containing 12 million of them. Inevitably, too, cases got bogged down in disputes over what was or was not legitimate accounting practice.[35] Even worse, much as with arms export law violations where the easiest defense lay in arguing that the government secretly approved of the shipment or was covertly doing the same thing, in procurement cases all that had to be shown was that the Pentagon itself had helped the contractors conspire to rig bids, cover up cost overruns or fake test results, and the case collapsed.

These problems were driven home forcibly in the attempted prosecution of General Dynamics. By the time it was arraigned, the country's largest arms maker had managed fifteen straight years of record profits without once being burdened with taxes - some years it even got a refund. This remarkable record could be partly explained if, as the prosecution contended, the company had, among many other things: committed multiple frauds in the construction of a special anti-aircraft gun that managed to blast hundreds of millions of dollars worth of holes in the defense budget while never firing a shot; overcharged by upwards of a billion dollars on its nuclear subs, of which only a tiny part could be accounted for by all the gifts it gave the admiral who god-parented the program; and bribed South Korean and Egyptian government officials to sell its fighters. Yet the prosecution was never able to penetrate the buddy system, crack the codes, access the secret defense department files or even understand whether the contract for the anti-aircraft gun was drawn up on a fixed-price or best-effort basis. If it were the latter, and the money ran out before the project was done, the company could discharge its legal responsibilities by delivering nothing much more than a bucket of bolts. The money did run out, the contract was canceled, General Dynamics was prosecuted; and the case ended with the government apologizing for daring to question the firm's integrity.[36]

Then, even when convictions were secured, the impact on the malefactor was negligible. Sundstrand, for example, pleaded guilty in the largest of all of the cost-padding cases, and paid nearly $200 million in fines. Yet all the officers of the company were cleared of fraud. The only really effective punishment would have been suspension from future participation. By the time the second round of defense cases ended in 1990, 25 of the 100 largest contractors had been found guilty of criminal fraud, yet not a single one was barred from further Pentagon business. Much like crimes committed by intelligence agents, each conviction was greeted with a plea from the defense department that the company's work was essential for national security.[37]

In any case, any prospects of seriously reforming the procurement system and punishing those that had abused it were defeated in Operation Desert Storm. In the euphoria of the 1992 victory by American armies over Iraq in the Middle East, and therefore over France and Russia, Iraq's main suppliers, in the world arms market, talk about useless weapons produced by conniving contractors using fraudulent methods ceased. President George Bush himself conferred on the system the ultimate accolade by choosing to give his victory speech while standing in front of a model of the latest high-tech military accomplishment, the Patriot anti-missile missile.

In reality, once the hype was stripped away, most of the damage to Iraq was actually done by the cheapest and oldest tanks and planes in the American arsenal. Furthermore, the performance of fancy new material was grossly exaggerated. Thus, the Patriot, although deployed against the easiest of all possible quarries, the ancient and slow SCUD, had a single warhead and lacked any inherent capacity to take evasive action, may well have made the situation even worse, by, for example, chasing bits and pieces of already destroyed missiles and then following debris into the ground, thus helping the incoming missiles strike their target.[38] Still, all this was overlooked in the blush of "victory" over an enemy totally unprepared psychologically or materially for combat. Indeed, in the subsequent 1991 Paris Air Show, where US high-tech equipment played a starring role, there were even US Air Force pilots, paid for by the Pentagon, standing beside their planes telling war stories to would-be buyers (Hartung 1994: 2-3, 12).

Along with a systematic effort by successive US governments to reduce restrictions on weapons sales, the result of the war was to confirm by a large measure the US in the position of number one international supplier of a commodity of which the world assuredly does not need more. The result was also to largely eliminate any serious questioning of the corporate and political culture that gave birth to the problem. Most of the remaining prosecutions were either buried or settled with plea-bargains that, beyond some marginal tinkering,[39] left the procurement system effectively intact.

Yet, in the final analysis, the storm and fury over procurement fraud was really akin to the aluminum chaff sprayed out by jet-fighters to deflect heat-seeking missiles fired either by the enemy or, in the case of American equipment, sometimes by their own side. It ignored four essential factors.

First, there was no proof that the military industries in the 1980s were intrinsically any more corrupt than the same era's Wall Street stock-brokers, Savings & Loan bankers, tele-evangelists or foreign policy planners in the Reagan-Bush White House. To a remarkable degree, contractor fraud simply reflected the prevailing economic ideology and the remarkable degree to which business performance in general had come to be judged less by long-term stable earnings than short-term speculative gains. Perhaps the only difference was that, for most people, to cite the old proverb, opportunity knocks only once; whereas military contractors were allowed to pound incessantly on the Treasury's front-door with their $436.00 claw hammers.

Second, the real problem was assuredly not corruption *per se* but the nature of the weapons procurement process itself, the fact that increasingly initiative came from the suppliers rather than the users, and the accommodating change in military career priorities so that procurement jobs were seen as more desirable than operations ones. That, in turn, meant that actual use, whether for offense or defense, was a secondary consideration. The fundamental objectives of the system had become profoundly commercial in nature.

Third, demands to clean up the system were based on a complete misunderstanding of a subtle but important transformation in the logic of

US arms expenditure that had occurred in the 1980s. In the Reagan-Bush era, in addition to the traditional role of military expenditure in macro-economic stabilization, it was increasingly seen as a fundamental tool of economic warfare with the USSR. The objective was to lock the Soviet Union into a military spending spree that would eventually drive it into bankruptcy.[40] In effect corporate crime and economic warfare had developed a symbiotic relationship. Once the main strategic purpose of military spending became not preparing to meet the USSR militarily but to destabilize it economically, then, in a backhanded way, profiteering was patriotic. And the real beauty of the CIA technique for measuring Soviet military spending was that every time a gross fraud was committed, driving up the cost of some item, the practice of imputing US prices to Soviet military spending automatically ratcheted up the estimate of that spending and provided a justification for the US to lavish yet more on its military the next year.

Fourth, it has never been clear why a clean and efficient Pentagon is supposed to be an improvement over the status quo. Much the way corrupt governments whose leaders spend their time stuffing money into Swiss bank accounts can sometimes be an improvement over those capable of carrying out ugly agendas with brutal efficiency, arguably in the case of military procurement, institutionalized fraud could in some ways be a blessing in disguise - the accompanying cost inflation meant that fewer weapons could be bought, and those that were would often fail to accomplish their objectives of destroying property and killing people.

ACKNOWLEDGMENTS

The author would like to thank the John D. and Catherine MacArthur Foundation for its financial support during the course of the research.

NOTES

[1]　This paper is derived from a larger research project investigating the operation of the modern arms black market. An enlarged version will appear shortly as a chapter in that study.

[2]　Some of these issues are explored in Naylor (1995 and 1996).

[3]　The still-unrivaled account of the primitive stage of American buccaneer capitalism, in the military and civil sectors, is by Myers (1907). The Morgan story (Myers 1907: 569) is also recounted in Lewisohn (1937: 129-31).

[4] Sampson (1977: 54-5). After two decades this still remains an excellent work, albeit most of its attention is focused on the 1960s and 1970s sales drives by the American aerospace companies.

[5] McCormick (1965: 19, 45-48, 109). This is the best of several biographies of Zaharoff, most of which are marred by either idolatry or the impulse to treat him as evil incarnate rather than just a product of his time and chosen profession.

[6] For the similar situation in Canada, see Naylor (1981).

[7] The carnage was particularly heavy from artillery barrages and massed machine-gun fire. But the main public revulsion was caused by poison gas attacks even though they only accounted for one third of one percent of the war dead.

[8] On an early investigation of the technology question see Reppy (1985). There had been a very active debate in the US concerning the extent to which the military-industrial system really has contributed to American prosperity. For the negatives the finest research has been by Melman (1974, 1984, and 1988). There is a useful summary of his views in *The Nation* 20/5/91. There is also a large body of literature strongly influenced by Melman, sometimes without proper acknowledgment. See, for example, Degrasse (1983) and Markusen and Yudken (1992). But see also the interesting critique by Doug Henwood in *Left Business Observer* 17/4/91, 3/6/91.

[9] The process of inflating Soviet military spending for electoral purposes was actually begun by Jimmy Carter who used it to justify a substantial hike in military expenditure. See Perlo (1980). But it was under Reagan it reached its apogee.

[10] The impact was assessed by Fitzgerald (1989: 76). He contends the result of dollarization alone was to immediately double the estimate of the size of Soviet military spending. The entire exercise is superlatively analyzed by Holzman (1990 and 1992).

[11] Nincic in *The Arms Race*, analyzed the spending patterns and came to an interesting conclusion. If the arms race had been genuinely prompted by one side reacting to what the other had, military expenditure by the two sides would have moved roughly in tandem. What one side got, the other must obtain, either more of it, or a fancier version. The reality was quite different. Over the course of the Cold War, military expenditures by the two expanded sometimes in tandem, sometimes independently, sometimes in the opposite direction, suggesting that domestic factors were the real explanation for the volume of and direction of changes in arms expenditure.

[12] This has been most effectively analyzed by Weiner (1990).

[13] The story is related in Boulton (1978) and in Sampson (1977).

[14] Yoshio Kodama's career is examined in Kaplan and Dubro (1986).

[15] See, for example, *Wall Street Journal* June 10, 1994.

[16] See the account of Fitzgerald (1989). Fitzgerald was brought into the Pentagon because of his experience as a cost-cutting manager in civil production. He went on to become the most celebrated of subsequent "whistle-blowers".

[17] On the accounting procedures, see O'Shea (1986).

[18] *New York Times* August 29, 1985, October 19, 1988, and October 24, 1988, *Business Week* September 26, 1988, and January 23, 1989.

[19] *New York Times* August 29, 1985.

[20] *Wall Street Journal* December 21, 1991.

[21] Rockwell, the country's second largest military contractor was caught several times falsifying time cards. When General Electric was found doing the same, the problem was dismissed as merely one of "technical violations".

[22] *The Wall Street Journal* October 29, 1985, and November 12, 1985.

[23] *Miami Herald* May 14, 1987. *New York Times* September 10, 1988, October 13, 1988, and January 27, 1989; *Business Week* September 26, 1988, and January 23, 1989.

[24] *New York Times* September 10, 1988, October 13, 1988, and January 27, 1989; *Business Week* September 26, 1988, and January 23, 1989.

[25] What passes for bidding in military contracting is really a travesty of the notion of confidential sealed tenders. In Pentagon-speak, it is called "negotiated competitive bidding" (Williams 1988: 45).

[26] *Business Week* July 4, 1988.

[27] *Business Week* July 4, 1988; *The Wall Street Journal* June 27, 1988.

[28] *Christian Science Monitor* March 30, 1989.

[29] *New York Times* July 7, 1988. The most notorious was Melvyn Paisley. See *Christian Science Monitor* June 27, 1988; *The Wall Street Journal* July 18, 1988, November 14, 1989, march 19, 1990; *Los Angeles Times* July 9, 1988; *New York Times* July 11, 1988, August 18, 1988, January 28, 1989, March 9, 1989, September 6, 1991 and Pasztor (1995).

[30] *New York Times* July 7, 1988; *The Wall Street Journal* July 7, 1988, September 30, 1988; *Washington Post* August 7, 1988. It was also pointed out that even if the plane had been an F-14, it was not designed to carry anti-ship missiles. At most it would have had to attack the USS Vincennes with "dumb bombs" which would have required it get so close and in such a position that the ship would have had ample time for visual identification.

[31] *New York Times* July 18, 1994.

[32] Williams, (1988: 28,45). Jewelry making was commonplace because the military industry absorbs as raw material huge amounts of precious metals and certain near-gem quality stones. And the decoders could be simply fashioned from the abundance of electronic components hanging about.

[33] *New York Times* August 28, 1987.

[34] *New York Times* March 16, 1989; *The Wall Street Journal* March 15, 1989.

[35] *The Wall Street Journal* October 11, 1990.

[36] *The Wall Street Journal* April 3, 1985, May 20, 1987, June 22, 1987, August 13, 1987; *Financial Times* April 3, 1985; *New York Times* May 22, 1985, May 30, 1985, July 30, 1990; *Business Week* March 25, 1985, August 22, 1988; *Fortune* April 28, 1986.

[37] *New York Times* November 12, 1990.

[38] Page, Williams, and Broll (1991); *New York Times* April 17, 1991.

[39] *Fortune* January 11, 1993.

[40] An interesting overview of the strategy of economic warfare is by Schweizer (1994).

REFERENCES

Boulton, David. (1978). *The Lockheed Papers*, London: Whitaker.

Degrasse, Robert W. (1983). *Military Expansion, Economic Decline*, New York: M. E. Sharpe.

Fitzgerald, A. Ernest. (1989). *The Pentagonists*, Boston: Independent Institute.

Hartung, William. (1994). *And Weapons For All*, New York: Harper Collins.

Holzman, Franklyn D. (1990). "How the CIA Distorted the Truth about Soviet Military Spending," *Challenge*, 33(2): 27-36.

_____. (1992). "The CIA's Military Spending Estimates: Deceit and Its Costs," *Challenge*, 35 (3): 28-39.

Howe, Russell Warren. (1980). *Weapons: the International Game of Arms, Money and Diplomacy*, New York: Doubleday.

Kaplan, David and Alec Dubro. (1986). *Yakuza*, New York: Addison Wesley.

Kaufman, Richard. (1970). *The War Profiteers*, New York: Bobbs-Merrill.

Knightley, Phillip. (1986). *The Second Oldest Profession*, London: Deutsch.

Lewisohn, Richard. (1937). *The Profits of War Through The Ages*, New York: Dutton.

Markusen, Ann and Joel Yudken. (1992). *Dismantling the Cold War Economy*, New York: Basic Books.

McCormick, Donald. (1965). *Peddler of Death: the Life of Sir Basil Zaharoff*, London.

Melman, Seymour. (1970). *Pentagon Capitalism*, New York: McGraw Hill.

_____. (1974). *The Permanent War Economy*, New York: Simon and Schuster.

_____. (1984). *Profits Without Production*, New York: Knopf.

_____. (1988). *The Demilitarized Society*, Montreal: Harret House.

Myers, Gustavus. (1907). *History of the Great American Fortunes*, New York: Random House.

Naylor, R. T. (1981). "The Canadian State, the Accumulation of Capital and the Great War," *Journal of Canadian Studies*, 16 (4): 26-55.

_____. (1995). "Loose Cannons: Covert Commerce and Underground Finance in the Modern Arms Black Market," *Crime, Law and Social Change*, 22: 1-57.

_____. (1996). "The Rise of the Modern Arms Black Market and the Fall of Supply Side Control" in Virginia Gamba (ed.) *Society Under Seige: Crime, Violence and Illegal Weapons*, South Africa: Institute for Security Studies, Halfway House.

Nincic, Miroslav. (1982). *The Arms Race: the Political Economy of Military Growth*, New York: Praeger Publishers.

O'Shea, James. (1986). "The real nuts and bolts of Pentagon contracts," *Bulletin of the Atomic Scientists*, 42: 19-20.

Overy, R.J. (1994). *War And Economy In The Third Reich*, Oxford: Clarendon Press.

Page, Kevin, Greg Williams, and Charles Broll. (1991). *High Tech Weapons in Desert Storm: Hype or Reality?* Washington D.C.: Project on Government Procurement.

Pasztor, Andy. (1995). *When The Pentagon Was For Sale*, New York: Scribner.

Perlo, Victor. (1980). "The Myth of Soviet Superiority," *The Nation*, September 13: 201, 214.

Reppy, Judith. (1985). "Military R&D and the civilian economy," *Bulletin of the Atomic Scientists*, 41: 10-41.

Sampson, Anthony. (1977). *The Arms Bazaar*, London: Hodder and Stoughton.

Schweizer, Peter. (1994). *Victory: The Reagan Administration's Secret Strategy That Hastened The Collapse Of The Soviet Union*, New York: Atlantic Monthly Press.

Thayer, George. (1969). *The War Business*, New York: Simon and Schuster.

Weiner, Tim. (1990). *Blank Check: The Pentagon's Black Budget*, New York: Warren Books.

Williams, Gregory. (1988). *Defense Procurement Papers, Campaign '88*, Washington D.C.: Project on Military Procurement.

4

CORRUPTION: QUANTITATIVE ESTIMATES

ARVIND K. JAIN
Concordia University

We have two objectives in this chapter. First, we would like to understand the quantitative impact of causes, consequences, and remedies of corruption. Second, we would like to get to know the methodologies that can be used to study the impact of corruption on other economic variables. Is the impact of corruption sufficiently large to merit further studies or is it small enough that it can be treated as being within the range that would be considered acceptable cost of any system?[1] Which of the factors that fester corruption have the most impact on its growth? Does corruption have an effect on the income distribution within societies - thus raising the question that cannot be answered by looking merely at growth rates? In what areas does corruption have a greater impact - on the level of income or on the distribution of income? Does corruption affect welfare of societies through investments and growth rates? Is it possible to identify and quantify the route through which corruption affects growth? Is it possible to identify sectors that systematically benefit or lose from corruption? What are the macro-economic variables on which corruption has the most impact? Which measures to combat corruption seem to be the most successful?

Not all of these questions have yet been studied. To answer some of the other questions, we will summarize past empirical studies on various aspects of corruption as well as of rent-seeking behavior. Empirical studies on corruption are of recent vintage; reliable estimates are just beginning to appear. There is, however, sufficient volume of existing work so that scholars and policy makers can begin to understand how important corruption might be. To facilitate future studies on corruption, this and the following chapters will introduce the reader to the variety of models, methodologies, and data sets that have been used in empirical studies on corruption and rent seeking. These studies are described in sufficient details so that the future scholars can focus rapidly on the most relevant past work. This chapter will focus on the work that links corruption to other variables. The next chapter will provide more details of the attempts to measure the independent variable common to these studies - the extent of corruption in various societies.

Past studies on corruption and rent-seeking may be organized in two ways. We could separate them by theme: does the study address the causes of corruption, or the impact of corruption on modern societies, or does it look at the efficacy of potential solutions. Past studies could also be divided according to the level at which the corrupt activity takes place. In this chapter, we will separate the past studies according to the latter criterion. Following the distinctions outlined in the Exhibit 1.1, we start with the studies of corruption at the political level, then consider the activities at the administrative and lower bureaucratic levels and finally examine the impact of some rent seeking activities. Although we will focus largely on summarizing studies of empirical estimates of corruption in this chapter, a few case studies that are pertinent will also be included.

A few of the studies described below may, in due time, come to be recognized as path breaking studies in the are of corruption. These studies include those by Mauro (1995, 1997) and Tanzi and Davoodi (1997). Since these studies have addressed some fundamental measurement issues in the field of corruption, they are relevant to the discussion of corruption from a number of perspectives. Hence, a number of writers in this book rely upon the conclusions of these studies. The reader is likely to have a sense of *déjà vu*. Such repetition, though regrettable, is unavoidable.

EFFECTS OF POLITICAL CORRUPTION

The highest level at which corruption can occur is at the level of political leadership. We are not familiar with any empirical study that has successfully quantified the cost of corruption at this level. There is, however, no dearth of qualitative studies and accounts, academic as well as journalistic, of how politicians use their powers to enrich themselves - whether in "law-abiding" and "democratic" societies or under "corrupt" and "dictatorial" regimes. A number of these studies document systematic corruption in specific countries, establishing links between the activities of individuals and firms on the one hand and government bureaucracies and political leadership on the other.

The main difficulty in linking corruption to the actions of the politicians in these studies has been the establishment of the causal link between the actions of the government elite and the acts of corruption. In most instances, decisions that create corrupt income for the decision makers also bring some economic benefits for the society. This raises the question of motivation for these acts. Are these actions motivated by a desire to enhance public welfare while, as a partial consequence, bringing some benefits for the bureaucrats and the politicians, or, are these actions motivated by the self-interest of the politicians but are couched in terms of some enhancement of public welfare? If politicians take the optimal decisions from the point of view of their clients - the populace - while ensuring that either they themselves or their close associates capture some of the gains resulting from these actions, the consequences of the corruption part of their decisions are likely to affect, *largely*, the distribution of income within the society. Instead of some members of the public receiving all the rents, the close associates of the politicians or the decision-makers receive some of those rents. If, on the other hand, politicians choose between alternatives proposals for investments and expenditures based on the criterion of self-gain, the consequences of the decisions are likely to affect, primarily, the pattern of resources allocation within the society and hence the growth rates of the economy. The consequences for the distribution of income within the society will be secondary in this case.

From the point of view of empirical studies, the difficulty is in establishing the cause and effect relationship between the actions of the decisions makers and the consequences of these decisions.[2] When the decisions result in some economic growth as well as in enrichment of decision makers, it becomes difficult to assign one or the other motivation to the decisions. It is difficult to show, in such cases, that the government's decisions would have been different if possibilities for earning corrupt income were not present.

A number of attempts, however, have been made to understand the link between the decisions taken by the politicians, economic growth, and corruption. Klitgaard (1990) documents the manner in which government leaders distort policy decisions to suit their own interests in one developing country. Klitgaard describes how political leaders, faced with a grim economic situation and advisors from international organizations that seem more concerned with their reports than with the realities of the country, make the best of the situation by expropriating country's wealth for themselves and their supporters. Naylor (1987 and 1990) provides descriptions of corruption under dictatorships in the third world, for example under Marcos in Philippines and Samoza in Nicaragua, as well as under democratic leaders in the industrialized countries. Recent estimates of the wealth of one of the most corrupt political leaders in the contemporary world, Mobutu Sese Seko of Zaire, reach as high as 9 billion dollars. Majul (1994) and Walger (1995) document the corruption among the political elite in Argentina in the post-military-dictatorship regime.

Corruption is not, of course, a problem of developing countries alone. Over the past few years, corruption scandals in Belgium, Italy, and Japan and shaken the political systems in these countries. Cameron (1994) has produced a detailed account of the corruption within the regime of Brian Mulroney, the Prime Minister of Canada till 1993. It is remarkable how the general public may have understood the nature of that regime: in the general elections following his departure, the party that he had led, the Conservative party, was able to win only two seats in the parliament. Since the fall of the communist regime in the Soviet Union, corruption in Russia at the highest level has become everyone's favorite example of how things tend to fall apart. Klitgaard (1998) remarks that whereas Venezuelans can produce a two-volume dictionary of corruption in their country, French are not far behind with a similar volume of their own.

Recently, two studies have examined the impact of corruption at the political level on public and private investments in an economy. Tanzi and Davoodi (1997) find that corruption motivates government leaders to increase public investments, which does not necessarily add to economic welfare. Mauro (1995 & 1997) finds that corruption affects the level of investment in the economy. These studies need to be discussed in details.

In what is perhaps the first quantitative estimate of the effects of corruption on the way decisions on public investments are made, Tanzi and Davoodi begin with an observation common to many countries where governments play a large role in the economy. The costs and the nature of public investment expenditures in these countries often defy common sense or economic rationale. Corruption - usually in the form of bribes - motivates decision-makers to direct public expenditure through channels that make it easier to collect corrupt income through bribes. This creates a bias towards large value and grand construction projects rather than value-enhancing maintenance expenditures or decentralized-small-scale projects. The authors hypothesize that the self-interest of corrupt officials will lead them to increase the level of public investment in their economy. They test their propositions with the help to two indices of corruption. The first, from *Business International*, is available for 68 countries for the1980-83 period. The second, in *International Country Risk Guide*, provides annual estimates of corruption between 1982 and 1995 for between 42 to 95 countries.

The empirical tests by Tanzi and Davoodi provide strong support for their propositions. Public investment as a ratio of GDP is strongly related to a corruption index. The relationship, moreover, remains strong even when corrections are made for the levels of development and of economies (proxied in this study by real per capita GDP) and for the availability of funds to finance large scale projects (measured here as government revenue to GDP ratio). The authors also examine the link between the quality of investments and corruption. They estimate the quality of investments by five proxy variables: percentage of total paved roads that are in good condition, electric power system losses as a percentage of total power output, faults in the telecommunication system, loss of water, and the percent of railway diesel engines that are kept in working condition. The authors find strong, and as expected negative, relationship between the level of corruption and how well the decision makers emphasize the maintenance of past projects. The study also finds that government revenue itself depends upon the level of corruption. As hypothesized, government revenue is found to decrease with the level of corruption since higher corruption is expected to be related to lower tax revenues - a proposition that is confirmed by Chand and Moene (see below).

The authors also find that higher expenditure on public projects is related to lower funding for operations and maintenance (O&M) expenditures, although there are problems with obtaining precise data for these expenditures. Decision-makers that benefit from corruption associated with large projects and construction related expenditures are likely to have a bias for decisions that discourage maintenance of existing projects. Deterioration of existing facilities will create a justification for new projects, thus creating new opportunities for corrupt income. Using a number of proxies for this category of expenditures, and examining some direct indicators of maintenance effectiveness, the authors find strong support for their hypotheses. When the O&M expenditures are proxied by "expenditures on other goods and services,"[3] there is some support for the authors' proposition. When "other wages and salaries" are used as a proxy for O&M expenditures, the authors find unambiguous support for their hypotheses.

These authors conclude that corruption "reduces growth by increasing public investment *while reducing its productivity* [emphasis in the original] ... (and) by increasing government consumption ... (and) by reducing the quality of existing infrastructure ... (and) by lowering government revenue ..." (p. 20).

In what was perhaps the first empirical study that linked macro-economic performance to an index of corruption, Mauro (1995) found that corruption lowers the level of investment in the economy, thus lowering growth rates. The author's purpose was to "... identify channels through which corruption and other institutional factors affect economic growth and to quantify the magnitude of these effects" (p. 682). Recognizing that efficiency of economic institutions is jointly determined with performance of the economy, the author used "ethnolinguistic fractionalization" as an instrument variable that would be exogenous to both - economic variables and institutional efficiency. He used nine indices developed by *Business International,* one of which is an estimate of corruption between 1980 and 1983 for 68 countries, to measure the institutional efficiency.

Mauro's (1995) results indicate that corruption significantly lowers the levels of investment in an economy. This is found to be true even when countries are separated into low-red-tape and high-red-tape countries. Significant relationship between corruption and lower investment rates even in low-red-tape countries challenges the idea that corruption can be helpful for development when it plays the role of "greasing the wheels of bureaucracy."

Mauro (1997) extended the study to a large group of countries and examined, in addition to the links between corruption and investments, the effects of corruption on the composition of government expenditures. Results with the larger sample size confirm Mauro's earlier results that corruption significantly affects economic growth and investments in the economy. Furthermore, "... when GDP per capita is controlled for, government expenditure on education is negatively and significantly associated with higher levels of corruption... Government expenditure on health is also found to be negatively and significantly associated with corruption" (p. 98). Mauro's analysis is based on a corruption index that is calculated as the average of the corruption indices of *Business International* and *International Country Risk Guide.* Two sources were used to estimate government expenditures: Barro (1991) and IMF's *Government Finance Statistics.* Mauro, contrary to the later study by Tanzi and Davoodi (1997), did not find a significant relationship between corruption and the capital expenditures of governments.

The most fundamental issue for assessing and combating political corruption may be the recognition that political and administrative elite, acting as agents for the population at large, may yield to the temptations that agents in those positions are offered. It may be worthwhile to summarize a study by Krueger (1996) that establishes the economic costs of *implicit* collusion between certain segments of a society and the government (the clients $\{C_{k+1} ... C_{k+p}\}$ and the agent A_0 in terms of the Exhibit 1.1), although she does not refer to this collusion as corruption. Krueger describes economic crises and problems in a number of countries, among others Mexico, Turkey, and Ghana, and reviews some macroeconomic policies of these countries. Trying to understand how these policies are formulated, the author questions the model of government as a "benevolent social guardian" that often underlies economic analyses. This view of government, with a long tradition in economics, is based on the premise that "… governments and civil servants in some sense were 'above the system' " (p. 55). Among other criticisms of this "benevolent social guardian" model, Krueger questions "… why it should be assumed that those in the public sector will not also seek their own self-interest" (p. 57). Furthermore, government policies will generate rents for certain sectors of the society and hence the pressures from those sectors to maintain such policies in place to safeguard those rents.

CONSEQUENCES OF ADMINISTRATIVE CORRUPTION

Political corruption in a country is most often accompanied by a corruption of the administrative mechanism of the country. We refer here not to individual bureaucrats asking for bribes of small favors to carry out their tasks, but an administration where some types of internal markets or mechanisms are developed in which all levels of a bureaucracy cooperate to increase their corruption-related earnings. Clearly, the distinction between the two can be arbitrary. For the purpose of assessment of empirical studies of corruption, however, this distinction may be useful. We first summarize studies that have dealt with systemic administrative corruption and then with studies that deal with cases of "bribery."

Wade (1985) reports on one of the first systematic studies of how a whole administrative system can fall apart when corruption becomes endemic. Wade examined how an "internal labor market" had developed within the irrigation department in one of the states in India. Different positions within this department offered different opportunities for earning illicit revenues for administrators. Positions were, thus, ranked according to their earning potential and candidates for these positions offered a portion of their anticipated illicit earnings to those with power to allocate the positions. Since there were many opportunities for all involved in these situations to renege on their promises, thus threatening future earnings of others or diminishing the value of past payments, the attention of the administrators was focused on developing and implementing mechanism that would protect their illicit earnings rather than carrying out their official duties. There were also incentives for the administrators to increase their illicit earnings above those which they may have "purchased." This could only have been done by diverting government revenues to tasks other than those for which they were allocated. Moreover, the illicit earnings could only have been earned if the required tasks were not carried out according to the expected standards. In addition, simple technical decisions were politicized to the extent that elected politicians were more interested in allocation of positions than in their legislative duties. The author points to a number of consequences of this system.

"Canal managers are under pressure to behave almost exactly contrary to the ostensible objectives of their job: instead of reducing water uncertainty, they artificially increase it if they wish to maximize bribe revenue; instead of maintaining the canals in good conditions, they leave large stretches of the canal unmaintained so as to save maintenance funds for other purposes. Agricultural officers are under pressure ... to adulterate the special inputs. ... The effects of the transfer system are not only economic ... (but) also the undermining of the workable authority of government" (pp. 485-486).

Chand and Moene (1997) provide an estimate of the effects of corruption associated with collection of taxes in one country facing economic crisis: Ghana. Ghanaian economy suffered economic decline during 1960s and 1970s due to "... adverse terms of trade and domestic policies..." resulting in price and income controls and in much of the economy being driven underground (p. 5). Tax evasion that followed the economy going underground resulted in collapse of tax revenues. The corruption of tax officials, of course, was part of the problem:

"The tax system became riddled with all sorts of devices that were used by fiscal officers to supplement their incomes. A prominent instrument was the use of tax clearance certificates, which were required for a growing range of transactions, for example, acquiring trading licenses, a passport, and so on. The tax and customs administration became increasingly disorganized. This manifested itself in several ways including haphazard storage of taxpayer files, which were in any case poorly organized, the mixing up of assessment and collection functions in the hands of the same officers..." (p. 6).

This corruption resulted in decline of total revenues and grants of the government from 15.0 percent of the GDP in 1973 to 5.6 percent in 1983. Of this total amount, tax revenue declined from 12.8 percent to 4.6 percent between these two years. Taxes on domestic goods as well as international trade declined to about one-third of their value (measured as ratios of GDP) over this period.

Johnson, Kaufmann and Zoido-Loabton (1998) examine the effect corruption will have on the existence of unofficial or "underground" economy. Corruption seems to be highly correlated with the extent of the unofficial economy within a country. Using data on the extent of underground economy collected at the World Bank, they find significant relationship between existence of the unofficial economy and a number of variables that measure the existence of regulations unfavorable to business, quality of bureaucracy, and discretionary powers of the bureaucrats. Business friendliness of the regulation is estimated by a measure provided by Heritage Foundation, regulatory discretion by Global Competitiveness Survey reports, and the quality of bureaucracy by a survey conducted by Political Risk Services. In addition, analysis using Global Competitiveness Survey's estimates of tax burden shows increasing levels of unofficial economy with increasing tax burden. When, however, Fraser Institute's top marginal tax rate is included in the analysis, it becomes apparent that what matters is how the tax system is administered, not only the tax rates.

A few studies that measure the effect of corruption, especially in the form of bribery, on other economic variables will be summarized in the following chapter. Beck, Maher, and Tschoegl (1991), Hines (1995), and Lambsdorff (1998) find significant relationships between US trade in various industries and existence of bribery. These authors test if Foreign Corrupt Practices Act of 1977 in the United States limits US firms' ability to compete in the international markets against firms from countries that permit payments of bribery. Wei (1997), however, provides arguments for why FCPA may not be such a handicap for the US firms: if they have competitive products, they may be able to avoid paying bribes by evoking the possibility of their exposure to penalties under the US laws. Some research has also been carried out to examine the influence of economic and/or political variables on the existence of corruption. As summarized in the following chapter, research by Ades and Di Tella (1995) shows that openness to international trade negatively affects the level of corruption. Similarly, Ades and Di Tella (1997) show that transparent government policies, especially procurement and equal fiscal treatment, lower the level of corruption.

Johnson, Kaufmann, and Shleifer (1997) investigate the importance of efficiency of tax regimes and the incentives for the "unofficial" economy to exist in former Soviet Union and Central and Eastern European countries. Although, strictly speaking, poor performance of tax regimes may be explained by factors other than corruption, their concern is with understanding the role that corruption might play in tax collections and hence in economic performance. They use World Bank's estimates of the share of unofficial economy which are derived from data on electricity consumption. They find that "[L]iberalization, privatization, fairer taxation, and fewer regulations are all associated with a smaller unofficial economy. Better provision of public goods to the official economy is associated with a relatively larger official economy" (page 196). Further analyses "...provide some support for the argument that total output, not just the official output, is reduced by excessive government intervention. At the same time, the results also suggest that the mafia provides firms that operate unofficially with public goods which, if not of so high a quality as those delivered by the state in the official sector, are certainly good enough for the unofficial economy to function" (page 205). Their empirical work is of interest not only for the conclusions it reaches but also for the wide variety of estimates they use to measure liberalization, privatization, fairness of the tax regimes and the political environment, including the fairness of the taxation system.

CONSEQUENCES OF RENT-SEEKING BEHAVIOR

As outlined in the second chapter, rent-seeking behavior can be distinguished from corruption on the grounds of legality and misuse of bureaucratic power. Most rent-seeking activities are legal and do not imply that administrators use their powers for personal gains. Yet they are interesting for the understanding of corruption since they involve attempts by individual actors to influence the direction of economic policy or its implementation.

In her seminal paper on the consequences of rent-seeking, Krueger (1974) argued that tariffs are a form of rent-seeking behavior and estimated the cost of protectionism in two countries, India and Turkey. Krueger summarized a number of estimates of the costs of rent-seeking behavior and found that rent-seeking activities are very costly for the economies. It was estimated that in India in 1964, import licenses were worth between 100 and 500 percent of their face value. Total cost of rents, including those from losses on public investments, import licenses, controlled commodities, credit rationing and (bribes) for railway shipments was estimated to be about 7.3 percent of the national income (p. 294.) Krueger quotes a study for Turkey for 1968 which estimated the cost of import licenses to be about 15 percent of the GNP. This value was derived from the difference between the retail costs of selected commodities and their import costs, after allowing for distribution costs.

Lopez and Pagoulatos (1994) also estimated the costs of tariffs. Using Harberger as well as Tullock/Posner estimates of costs of trade and competition barriers for a large number of food and tobacco industries in the United States, they find that social cost of these "barriers amounts to approximately 12.5 percent of domestic consumption" (p. 158). Their tests indicate that about two-thirds of these losses can be attributed to the activities related to political action committees.[4]

Mixon, Laband and Ekelund (1994) examine the implications for resource allocation of legislators accepting perquisites, specifically entertainment at restaurants, whose value may be difficult to quantify. They hypothesize that "(W)hen allowance is made for (approximate) per capita income and other key variables, state capital cities [in the United States] will contain a larger per capita percentage of sit-down (non-fast food) restaurants than paired randomly-chosen same-state cities with similar income characteristics" (p. 173). Their empirical tests, based upon regressions of number of restaurants on population, a dummy variable for state capitals, income, and distance from the nearest coastline, support their hypothesis.

Lenway, Morck and Yeung (1996) examined one industry in details to understand the consequences of rent-seeking behavior on the stock-holders, the managers, and the workers in the industry. Steel industry in the United States has faced threats of foreign competition for a long time. During the 1970s and the 1980s, many firms in the industry successfully lobbied the government to obtain protection from Japanese and European competition through "trigger price mechanism" and voluntary export restraints. The rationale for such demands was that temporary protection against foreign competition will allow domestic firms time to restructure and become competitive. The authors examine whether such protectionism helped the firms re-tool and become competitive or merely created extra rents for various interested parties within the industry. The focus of their analyses is the consequences of the trigger price mechanisms in 1977 and 1980 and the voluntary export restraints in 1982 and 1984.

The authors find that within the steel industry, the firms that sought protection were different from those that did not lobby for protection in terms of their sizes, specialization within the industry, returns, growth rates, and R&D spending. A "lobbying" firm was defined as one that filed a petition for protection, complained about foreign practices, or testified in support of protection in the congress during the study period. Lobbying firms were found to be different from non-lobbying firms. For the study period, non-lobbying firms were smaller, were less concentrated on steel, provided higher returns on their assets, had higher growth rate for their sales, and spent more on R&D. Workers as well as the CEOs at the lobbying firms were found to earn more than at non-lobbying firms.

The effect of protectionism on the shareholders was estimated as the cumulative abnormal return on the stocks of their firms over the period when the protectionist measures were being announced by the government. The lobbying firms' stockholders were found to have earned abnormal returns in three of the four announcements. The authors conjecture that the negative reaction for the fourth announcement probably reflects

"...investors' disappointment at the lower trigger prices (than expected)" (p. 416). Since the non-lobbying firms obtain a free ride with these announcements, they also earn abnormal returns in some of these instances, although less than the lobbying firms. The authors believe that the different returns are possible because "[L]obbyers may have grown more adept at politically engineering trade barriers specifically favorable to themselves, but may also have undermined non-lobbyers' investments in innovations" (p. 420).

The authors are also able to show that the labor as well as the managers of the lobbying firms gains from the rent seeking activities in the steel industry. Mean wages for lobbying firms increased by 1.5% per year after the 1984 restrictions whereas those for non-lobbying firms fell by (significantly different) 1.6% per year. Total employment for lobbying firms declined whereas that for non-lobbying firms increased. The total compensations for top managers show similar patterns. The compensation for the CEOs of the lobbying firms increased after 1984 whereas there was no change in the compensation of the CEOs of non-lobbying firms.

Lenway, Morck and Yeung (1996) study shows quite clearly that firm engage in rent seeking behavior. Such behavior seems to benefit the owners, the managers, and the labor - at least in the case of the steel industry. Since the authors were not concerned with the costs of rent seeking activities, this study by itself does not answer the question of whether investment in rent seeking activities provides positive returns. We will need to know the cost of lobbying as well as the returns that the owners, the managers and the labor would obtain in the absence of protection. Studies on the activities of political action committees summarized below may provide some indications of these costs.

Recently, Stanbury (1998) has estimated the costs of supply restrictions generally negotiated by producers' lobby groups. He examined the values of quotas given by Dairy Farmers of Ontario to milk producers in three provinces of Canada. These quotas allow farmers to sell milk at controlled prices in perpetuity. The result of these price controls is that milk sells at about Canadian $ 0.36/liter above its price in the United States in areas close to the Canadian border. Given the price at which these quotas trade in the secondary market, a farmer holding a quota recoups the investment in a quota in less than five years (ignoring the present value of the cash flows) while retaining the quota for the future as well as the right to sell the quota in the market.[5] These quotas, introduced by the federal and provincial governments in Canada in response to lobbying by the producers, result in Canadian consumers paying about 42 percent more for milk than their southern neighbors (p. 5). At the retail prices in March 1998, the total transfer from the consumers to producers would have amounted to about Canadian $ 2.8 billion at 1996-97 production volume.[6]

Beck and Connolly (1996), however, provide evidence of absence of rents associated with government announcements of favorable announcements. The authors look for gains for firms in Canada when government makes an announcement regarding a grant or a regulation that is expected to benefit the firm. They examine 48 events and measure stock price returns around the event date. Based on an absence of any abnormal returns, they conclude that firms do not gain from these events. They claim that the governments offer these incentives but manage to keep the gains for themselves.

Political Action Committees in the United States

Do economic actors - specifically profit-making firms - believe that they can influence the legislative process at a cost? In the United States, interest groups are allowed to form political action committees, or PACs, for the specific purpose of influencing legislation. Most PACs collect money from their members and channel these funds to legislators in the US Congress or the US Senate that they believe are likely to influence the outcome on pieces of legislation that are of interest to the interest group. PAC contributions are a legal way for members of PACs to obtain access to the legislators in order to appraise them of the members' interests in forthcoming legislation. Although a large number of studies have examined PAC contributions, we summarize two of these to demonstrate the link between contributions and rent-seeking behavior as well as to illustrate the methodologies used in these studies. One of the studies dealing with PACs (Lopez and Pagoulatos 1994) was included with the studies on rent seeking since it pertains more to the consequences of rent seeking behavior than to the process of contribution to PACs.

Bennett and Loucks (1994: 103) attempt to "... determine whether the [finance and saving and loan] industry attempts to influence policy outcomes by disproportionately contributing to members of the House banking committee, the committee with oversight responsibility from the finance and savings and loan industry." They examine the relationship between total contributions from either finance or savings and loan PACs to individual members of the US House of Representatives and the following independent variables: tenure of the member in the house which is measured by the number of years the member has been in the house, the legislator's margin of victory in the previous election, ideology of the legislator which is measured by the rating of the legislator by Americans for

Democratic Action, the party to which the legislator belongs, whether or not the legislator is a member of the House Banking Committee and whether or not the legislator is the chair of that committee. Tests for 1984, 1986, and 1988 election cycles reveal a significant relationship between the contributions and the memberships as well as the chairmanship of the banking committee. The authors find that the "members of the House banking committee receive significantly larger contributions from the finance and savings and loan industry than do other members of the Congress. Being a chairman of the [committee] also pays a dividend" (p. 103). A further study by Loucks (1996) confirms the relationship for the US Senate.

These studies, and others on this theme, provide clear evidence that firms are willing to pay to have access to the legislators. To prove that these expenditures are well spent, we will have to show that the contributions affected legislation and estimate the benefits derived from the change in the legislation. The cost of these contribution to the contributing firms, however, would appear to be small. The largest expenditure any PAC incurred in 1988 was $780,650 (Bennett and Loucks 1994: 94). The largest contributions received by one member of the congress was $184,400 in 1988 by F. J. St. Germain (Bennett and Loucks 1994: 100).

The studies on rent seeking behavior establish quite clearly that individuals and firms believe that they can gain from rent seeking activities and hence they are willing to invest resources in these activities. It is also clear that they are successful in influencing the legislation. Furthermore, studies provide evidence that rent seekers benefit from their activities. In so far as these activities represent dead-weight costs, the economy as whole ioses because of the existence of these activities.

SOLUTIONS FOR CORRUPTION

There is perhaps only one study that provides a quantitative estimate of whether certain solutions will work or not. Van Rijckeghem and Weder (1997) examine if the level of wages paid to public sector employees influence the level of corruption among these employees. If the relationship between these two variables were to be positive, one solution to corruption would involve ensuring that government employees were paid adequate wages. Using the corruption index derived from Political Risk Services' International Country Risk Guide, the authors examine the relationship between corruption and pay, internal as well as external controls, and distortions in the economy. The pay variable is measured as the ratio of government wages relative to manufacturing wages. The internal control variable is the index of "quality of bureaucracy" available from International Country Risk Guide. This index indicates "autonomy from political pressure" and "strength and expertise to govern without drastic changes in policy or interruptions in government services" as well as the existence of an "established mechanism for recruiting and training." Several proxies were used to measure the variable "external controls." These proxies included "rule of law," "political rights and civil liberties," and "PPP adjusted per capita GDP and secondary school enrollment." Black market premium for foreign exchange rate provided a proxy for the distortions in the economy. The authors would have liked to include a measure of " statutory penalty rate" and a measure of cultural factors or a lack of leadership. Since measurements for these variables were not available, they were not included in the study.

Empirical results show "a close negative association between relative civil wages and corruption across the developing countries…" The authors "…tend to reject the hypothesis that higher pay leads to reduced corruption in the short run, … The "quality of bureaucracy" and the black market premium are significant in the within regressions, though the latter is not economically significant" (pp. 31, 34). Based on the analysis, the authors are not able to differentiate empirically between an efficiency or a fair wage hypothesis (that higher wages will reduce corruption by tilting the balance in the favor of cost of penalties when corrupt officials weigh the extra income from corruption against costs of penalties) and a shirking model (in which income from bribery is so high that wages have no influence on the level of corruption). The study points to a number of conclusions that may be important from the point of fighting corruption.

"First, an increase in the ratio of civil service to manufacturing pay from 1 to 2 is associated with an improvement in the corruption index (which ranges from 0 to 6) on the order of 1 point in the "between" (i.e., cross-country) regressions for a sample of 25 developing countries. Second, civil service wages are highly correlated with measures of rule of law and quality of bureaucracy, and may therefore have additional indirect effects on corruption. Third, relative pay has no significant effect on corruption in "within country" regressions, indicating that pay may not have a contemporaneous effect on corruption. Fourth, quasi-eradication of corruption requires a relative wage of 3-7 times the manufacturing wage. Stronger internal and external controls are associated with lower corruption across countries" (p. 4).

CONCLUDING REMARKS

The range of quantitative studies included in this chapter point to the potential as well as the problems associated with the measurement of causes, consequences, and remedies of corruption. The largest problem will continue, for the foreseeable future at least, to be the measurement of the dependent variable – corruption. There are at least three issues to be addressed here. First, We need a consistent measure of corruption. Lambsdorff in the following chapter describes the attempts of Transparency International to develop one such index. Second, we need to be able to differentiate between different types of corruption. Tanzi and Kaufmann in their chapters in this volume discuss why corruption cannot be seen as one uniform phenomenon and why subtle differences between various forms of corruption have to be recognized. Third, most empirical studies will need a time series on corruption. It is not enough to have a measure of corruption at one point in time. Clearly corruption levels within countries change over time. Other problems with empirical studies on corruption are common to all areas of research: we need clear models and measurements of independent variables.

ACKNOWLEDGEMENTS

The author is grateful to the Social Sciences and Humanities Research Council, Ottawa, for a grant that made this research possible.

NOTES

[1]   In the words of Rose-Ackerman (1997: 33): "In seeking realistic reform it is important to realize that, like all illegal activities, the efficient level of bribery is not zero. Bribery is costly to control. Reform must consider the marginal costs as well as the marginal benefits of anticorruption strategies."

[2]   See Mauro (1997: 102-104) for the importance of causality between corruption and the government expenditure on education.

[3]   They use data from Government Finance Statistics, IMF.

[4]   See the section below on other research relating to the activities of these committees, known as PACs.

[5]   In March 1998, the quota was selling for $ 16,501 per kg. of butterfat. Since it takes 100 liters of milk to produce 3.6 kg. of butter, the farmer acquires a right to sell 100/3.6 or 27.78 liters of milk every day. At the estimated price differential of $0.36/liter, the

farmers earn 10 dollars per day due to the quota. The cost of the quota is, therefore, recouped in 1650 days.

[6] This value is calculated as the extra payments for the 1996-97 production volume of 77.5 million hectoliters of milk (p. 11) at the per liter retail price difference between the United States and Canada.

REFERENCES

Ades, A. and R. Di Tella. (1995). "Competition and Corruption." Draft Paper, Keble College, Oxford University.

_____. (1997). "National Champions and Corruption: Some Unpleasant Interventionist Arithmetic." *The Economic Journal* 107: 1023-1042.

Barro, Robert. (1991). "Government Spending in a Simple Model of Endogenous Growth." *Journal of Political Economy*, 98 (5, part2): S103-25.

Beck, P.J., M.W. Maher and A.E. Tschoegl. (1991). "The Impact of the Foreign Corrupt Practices Act on US Exports." *Managerial and Decision Economics,* 12: 295–303.

Beck, R. L. and J. M. Connolly. (1996). "Some Empirical Evidence on Rent-Seeking." *Public Choice,* 87(1-2): 19-33.

Bennett, R. W. and C. Loucks. (1994). "Savings and loan and finance industry PAC contributions to incumbent members of the House Banking Committee." *Public Choice,* 79: 83-104.

Cameron, Stevie. (1994). *On The Take: Crime, Corruption, And Greed In The Mulroney Years,* Toronto: MacFarlane Walter and Ross.

Chand, Sheetal K. and Karl O. Moene. (1997). "Controlling Fiscal Corruption." *IMF Working paper* WP/97/100.

Hines, J.R. (1995). "Forbidden Payment: Foreign Bribery and American Business after 1977." Washington D.C.: National Bureau of Economic Research Working Paper, no. 5266.

Klitgaard, Robert. (1990). *Tropical Gangsters,* New York: Basic Books.

_____. (1998). "Roles for International Organizations in the Fight against Corruption," paper presented at the XIIIth International Congress of the International Society of Social Defence, Lecce, Italy, November 28-30.

Krueger, Anne Osborne. (1974). "The Political Economy of the Rent-Seeking Society," *American Economic Review,* 64: 291-303.

_____. (1993). *Political Economy Of Policy Reform In Developing Countries*, Mass: MIT press.

Lambsdorff, J. Graf. (1998). "An Empirical Investigation of Bribery in International Trade." *European Journal of Development Research*, 11(1): 40-59.

Lenway, Stefanie, Randall Morck, and Bernard Yeung. (1996). "Rent Seeking, Protectionism and Innovation in the American Steel Industry," *The Economic Journal*, 106: 410-421.

Lopez, Rigoberto A. and Emilio Pagoulatos. (1994). "Rent seeking and the welfare costs of trade barriers," *Public Choice*, 79(1-2): 149-160.

Loucks, Christine. (1996). "Finance Industry PAC Contributions to US Senators, 1983-88," *Public Choice*, 89: 219-229.

Majul, Luis. (1994). *Los Duenos de la Argentina: La Cara Oculta de los Negocios*, Buenos Aires: Editorial Sudamericana.

Mauro, Paolo. (1995). "Corruption and Growth," *Quarterly Journal of Economics*, 110(3): 681-712.

_____. (1997). "The Effects of Corruption on Growth, Investment, and Government Expenditure: A Cross–Country Analysis," in Kimberly Ann Elliot (ed.), *Corruption and the Global Economy*, Washington D.C.: Institute for International Economics, 83–107.

Mixon, F. G., Jr., D. N. Laband and R. B. Ekelund Jr. (1994). "Rent seeking and hidden in-kind resource distortion: Some empirical evidence," *Public Choice*, 78(2): 171-186.

Naylor, R.T. (1987). *Hot Money and The Politics of Debt.* Toronto: McClelland and Stewart.

_____. (1990). *Bankers, Bagmen and Bandits: Business and Politics in the Age of Greed*, Montreal: Black Rose Books.

Rose-Ackerman, Susan. (1997). "The Political Economy of Corruption," in Kimberly Ann Elliot (ed.), *Corruption and the Global Economy*, Washington D.C.: Institute for International Economics, 31-60.

Stanbury, W. T. (1998). "The Property Rights Implications of Supply Management and Marketing Boards," paper presented at Canadian Property Rights Research Institute conference on *Recognizing the Importance of Property Rights*, Calgary.

Tanzi, V. and Davoodi, H. (1997). "Corruption, Public Investment, and Growth." IMF Working Paper WP/97/139.

Van Rijckeghem, C., and Beatrice Weder. (1997). "Corruption and the Role of Temptation: Do Low Wages in Civil Service Cause Corruption?" IMF Working Paper, WP/97/73.

Wade, Robert. (1985). "The market for public office: Why the Indian state is not better at development" *World Development*, 13 (4): 467-97.

Walger, Sylvina. (1995). *Pizza Con Champan*, Buenos Aires: Espasa Calpe.

Wei, S. J. (1997). "How Taxing is Corruption on International Investors." Washington D.C.: NBER Working Paper 6030.

5
CORRUPTION IN COMPARATIVE PERCEPTION

JOHANN GRAF LAMBSDORFF
Universität Göttingen

ASSESSING THE CURRENT STAGE OF RESEARCH

Empirical research about corruption is quite a new undertaking. In an attempt to determine the causes and consequences of corruption academics have lately concentrated on cross–country analysis. At the center is mostly the use of some professional assessment of the degree of corruption in various countries. Such assessments are sometimes conducted by agencies in an attempt to determine country risks and sold to investors. Other sources such as surveys have been conducted in recent years and contributed to a cross–country assessment of the extent of corruption. These data have been fruitfully applied to the investigations about the following relationships.

Investment and Growth

There has been an extensive debate whether corruption "greases the wheels" by enabling individuals to avoid bureaucratic delays, or whether it "sands the wheels", mainly by lowering the security of property rights and by misallocation of resources. One possible empirical approach to this problem is by investigating the impact of corruption on investment and growth. The first systematic attempt for a sample of 67 countries has been undertaken by Mauro (1995). He finds that corruption lowers investment and thereby reduces growth. He claims that if Bangladesh were to improve the integrity of its bureaucracy to the level of that of Uruguay, its investment rate would increase by almost five percent of GDP. Similar results have been obtained by Knack and Keefer (1995) who incorporate corruption among other explanatory variables into one single index of institutional quality. Referring to the results of a private sector survey for a sample of 41 countries, Brunetti Kisunko and Weder (1997, p. 23 and 25) also supported these results. Similar to Mauro they find that there is no significant proof that corruption affects growth directly. However, it significantly reduces the investment-GDP ratio and thereby also reduces the growth level. Mauro (1997) provides further support for the results by referring to a larger sample of 94 countries. Yet the relationship between investment and corruption may be more complicated than stated above. Corruption may also raise the investment-GDP ratio since those who allocate resources may have better opportunities to extract illegal income from large investment projects as opposed to small labor contracts. Public investments are particularly susceptible to this kind of inefficient allocation and Mauro suggest that corruption may have a negative impact only on private investments. The overall corruption–investment relationship may thus underestimate the harmful effects of corruption and, in fact, even a positive impact of corruption on investment could indicate that corruption is harmful by "greasing the wrong wheels". This idea has been picked up by Tanzi and Davoodi (1997). Referring to panel data on corruption provided by the Political Risk Service for 1980–95 they suggest that corruption increases public investment while lowering the quality of the resulting infrastructure as measured by the condition of paved roads and power outages. The authors support their hypothesis by reporting a high significance of their statistical results. Yet, since the problem of serial correlation in the panel data (i.e. the low year-to-year variation of levels of corruption) is not adequately identified, the empirical evidence remains suggestive. A more direct method to disprove the notion of corruption as greasing the wheels is presented by Kaufmann (1997), by suggesting a positive correlation between corruption and the management time spent with bureaucrats.

Predictability of Corruption

A criticism of the Mauro results has been voiced by Wedeman (1996). He argues that while the correlation between corruption and the investment-GDP ratio might be strong for countries with little corruption, it looses power for countries with higher levels of corruption.[1] Therefore, he concludes that different kinds of corruption might be more decisive to growth and investment than the overall level of corruption as such. In a similar perspective World Development Report (1997) quotes an entrepreneur arguing "there are two kinds of corruption. The first one where you pay the regular price and you get what you want. The second is one where you pay what you have agreed to pay and you go home and lie awake every night worrying whether you will get it or if somebody is going to blackmail you instead." Referring to an index of the "predictability of corruption", obtained from a private sector survey, they suggest for a sample of 39 industrial and developing countries that for a given level of corruption, countries with more predictable corruption have higher investment rates. However, the World Bank restricted itself not to release any individual country data. This does not only impede future research in this area but somewhat limits the credibility of the results.

Government Expenditure

Mauro (1995 and 1997) investigates the effects of corruption on the composition of government expenditure and finds out that corruption lowers the expenditure on education, arguing that other expenditures offer better possibilities to collect bribes. His results are fairly robust to the use of alternative data or inclusion of other explanatory variables but may suffer a little from the low explanatory power of the regressions.[2] As mentioned above, it is widely believed that corruption leads to high government expenditures on capital and even to useless "white–elephant projects". However, his regressions do not provide significant evidence for this.

Foreign Direct Investments (FDI)

In an early attempt, Wheeler and Mody (1992) did not find a significant correlation between the size of FDI and the host country's risk factor -- which includes corruption among other variables and is highly correlated with corruption. More recently, a significant negative impact has been detected by Wei (1997), focusing on bilateral flows between 14 source and 45 host countries in 1990 and 1991. He finds that an increase in the corruption level from that of Singapore to that of Mexico is equivalent to raising the tax rate by over twenty percentage points. The robustness of his results might be questioned, however. Since his conclusions refer only to the overall performance of host countries in attracting FDI, it is straightforward to assume the error terms of the bilateral flows into one host country to be correlated with each other. This can inflate the significance levels he reports. Yet, in contrast to Wheeler and Mody (1992) his approach adequately includes the geographic distance as an explanatory variable. Another research has been undertaken by Hines (1995) who proves that US investors differed from others in preferring to locate their FDI in less-corrupt countries after 1977, due to the imposition of the Foreign Corrupt Practices Act (FCPA).

International Trade

In the first inquiry of its type, Beck, Maher and Tschoegl (1991) found a small but still significant impact of corruption on the export competitiveness of the USA as a result of the FCPA. Similar conclusions are provided by Hines (1995) proving a negative influence of corruption after 1977 on the US share of aircraft imports. These results are however insufficient in proving a competitive disadvantage for the USA, since they could just as well indicate that competitive advantages in corrupt marketplaces before 1977 had been neutralized thereafter. In order to adequately address this question in a broad research I investigated bilateral trade data between 1992 and 1995 for the leading 18 exporting and 87 importing countries (Lambsdorff, 1998). While controlling for common languages, geographic distance, export composition and trade blocks, I concluded that while Belgium, France, Italy, the Netherlands and South Korea have competitive advantages in countries perceived to be corrupt, disadvantages are obtained for Australia, Sweden and Malaysia. The USA also has significantly less market shares in corrupt countries than the other countries mentioned above. I suggest that these differences should be explained by different propensities of exporters to offer bribes and that the results propose that exporting countries have to share part of the responsibility for the level of bribery in international trade.

The Impact of Competition on Corruption

Concerning the causes of corruption it has been investigated, in how far corruption can be explained by the extent of rents which are prevalent in the private sector. Ades and Di Tella (1995) show for a sample of 55 countries that the share of imports to GDP negatively affects the level of corruption. Their results are robust to the inclusion of further explanatory variables and the use of alternative data for corruption with a different sample of countries. They conclude that economic competition as measured by the degree of a country's openness reduces corruption by lowering the rents which can possibly be extracted by state institutions. However, this kind of measure is not wholly convincing, since larger countries may have advantages in substituting a low import–GDP ratio by competition within their own country. A similar impact on the level of corruption is found for a (subjective) index of Market Dominance (which measures the extent to which dominance by a limited number of firms is detrimental to new business development) and an index of Anti–Trust Laws (which measures the effectiveness of anti–trust laws in checking non–competitiveness practices). Again, the authors conclude that the less competitive a market environment, the higher will be the amount of corruption by giving bureaucrats - the authors may have forgotten about the role of politicians in this respect - the incentive to extract some of the monopoly rents through bribes. However, the problem of causality has to be highlighted here: Corruption may also cause the restriction of market forces, since corrupt bureaucrats and politicians have an encompassing interest in high monopoly rents. The authors are addressing this problem with the help of instrumental variables, however, in how far these can actually considered to be exogenous to the problem might be open to criticism.

The Impact of Political Institutions on the Level of Corruption

For a sample of 32 countries Ades and Di Tella (1997) make use of an index that measures "the extent to which public procurement is open to foreign bidders" and another index that measures" the extent to which there is equal fiscal treatment to all enterprises". They suggest that both variables have a negative impact on the level of corruption. However, the sample of countries appears rather limited and the problem of causality not convincingly solved.[3] A similar correlation between corruption and policy distortion for 39 countries is presented in World Development Report (1997, pp. 104 and 168). Yet, since no further explanatory variables are included such an approach risks reporting spurious correlation and fails to even address the problem of causality. A more useful approach from World Development Report (1997, pp. 104 and 168) focuses on the quality of the judiciary. While controlling for other explanatory variables, an index of the predictability of the judiciary from a private sector survey significantly influences the level of corruption in 59 countries. A similar correlation between corruption and the independence of the judicial system is proposed in Ades and Di Tella (1996). Another less technical line of research took a corruption index as a starting point to illustrate the impact of political institutions on corruption. Noteworthy among others is the contribution by Heidenheimer (1996).

Recruitment, Salaries and the Level of Corruption

The impact of merit based recruitment on corruption in 35 developing countries has been investigated by Evans and Rauch (1996). Higher values of the merit based recruitment index are associated with a greater proportion of higher–level officials in the core economic agencies entering the civil service through a formal examination system, and that a higher proportion of those who did not enter through examinations have university degrees. While controlling for income, this index is negatively associated with corruption. In how far the level of public sector salaries contributes to the extent of corruption has been investigated by Van Rijckeghem and Weder (1997). They argue that low salaries force public servants to supplement their incomes illicitly while high salaries imply higher losses when getting caught. They find a significant negative influence of civil service wages relative to manufacturing wages on the level of corruption in a sample of 28 developing countries. Increasing the civil service wage from 1 to 2 will improve the corruption index by the order of 2 points of our index.[4] By acknowledging the existence of more indirect effects, the impact might be even larger. Yet, the authors are very careful in addressing the problem of causality: Corrupt countries tend to have a poor budgetary performance or may subscribe to the view that civil servants earn sufficient income from corruption and may reduce civil service pay as a consequence.

Miscellany

Formulated with less academic rigor, the media has been engaged in suggesting various correlation between corruption and human development, competitiveness, judicial quality, credit ratings or the spread of newspapers.[5] Since mostly other explanatory variables are missing, however, such correlation sometimes risk being misleading in the sense that they present spurious correlation.

A major disadvantage of the current state of research is that each contribution usually makes use of a different set of data. This does not only confuse readers but also limits the possibilities for direct comparisons between the various investigations. While some researchers used the 1980 data by Business International, others focused on more recent data obtained by the World Competitiveness Yearbook or the Political Risk Service. Each of the sources however may have its particular weaknesses and naturally raises problems of reliability and validity. On the other hand, some sources though reliable do not include enough countries for a fruitful use in empirical tests. These difficulties can be overcome or at least reduced by combining the existing sources into a combined index. Small surveys can be fruitfully introduced into empirical research while the reliability and validity can be strengthened by the standardization and combination into a single survey. This approach introduced for the creation of the Transparency International (TI) Corruption Perception Index in 1995[6] has been particularly endorsed by Lancaster and Montinola (1997). This may have been the reason for several up–to–date investigations to prefer the TI–index as opposed to any other single source. However, with 52 countries in the 1997 TI–index, the number of countries is somewhat limited and may be too small for some investigations.

The purpose of this contribution is to provide a reliable and extensive set of data of the perceived level of corruption as an indicator for real levels of corruption. This Corruption Perception Index (CPI) covers 101 countries and may be used for future empirical research. In addition to the 52 countries reported 1997 by TI we are assessing another 49 countries by applying the same technique. The reason they have been omitted in the official TI–publication is due to reliability: At least four sources were required for a country to be included there. We also report countries that have been subject of two or three sources. Of course, the reliability in such cases is sometimes lower. However, the number of sources is not the only measurement of reliability. The variance of the sources can also indicate the quality of an individual figure. Moreover, each investigation has its own reliability problems: Countries with reliable corruption figures may have less reliable data on other subjects of the investigation or may be of lower value for a particular investigation. For example, investigating the mineral sector may be of limited use if Saudi Arabia is not included into the sample and the slightly lower reliability of the corruption figure may thus be justified. The presentation of a complete table of corruption data as perceived by businesspeople, political analysts and the general public is intended to allow researchers to determine for themselves the appropriate sample of countries and to address the problem and reliability according to the particular needs of their investigation.

The appendix presents the Corruption Perception Index (CPI). This index is not an assessment of the corruption level in any country as made by ourselves, rather it is an attempt to assess the level at which corruption is perceived by businesspeople, political analysts and the general public. The index is a "poll of polls" and has been prepared using seven sources, including two surveys from the Institute for Management Development in Lausanne, Switzerland (World Competitiveness Yearbook), one from the Political & Economic Risk Consultancy Ltd. in Hong Kong (Asian Intelligence Issue #482), one by Gallup International (50th Anniversary Survey), two assessments by DRI/McGraw Hill (Global Risk Service) and the Political Risk Services, East Syracuse, New York (International Country Risk Guide), and finally a survey conducted by us at Göttingen University via internet (Internet Corruption Perception Index to be obtained via http://www.uni-goettingen.de/~uwvw) which gives contributors the possibility for anonymous contributions and also directly approaches employees of multinational firms and institutions. A complete list of the sources is provided in the appendix 5.2.

THE VALIDITY OF OUR APPROACH

Corruption is generally defined as the misuse of public power for private benefits, e.g., bribing of public officials, taking kickbacks in public procurement or embezzling public funds. With only little variation all our sources attempt to measure activities very close to this definition. The index tries to assess the degree to which public officials and politicians in particular countries are involved in corrupt practices. However, each survey collects subjective assessments and does not collect objective data. This is due to the fact that an objective approach is almost impossible. Corruption involves concealed actions and data are not revealed publicly. Objective data may be deduced from publications of the judiciary or the media. However, these data give an impression on how effective the media is in discovering and reporting about scandals and how independent and well trained the judiciary is in prosecuting. An efficient and incorruptible jurisdiction may bring about high numbers of convictions. Instead of acknowledging this, "objective" data would "punish" such a country with a bad score.

The precise perception of corruption might depend on the particular cultural background of respondents. As Bayley (1970) noted:

> "The western observer is faced with an uncomfortable choice. He can adhere to the Western definition, in which case he lays himself open to the charge of being censorious ... On the other hand, he may face up to the fact that corruption, if it requires moral censure, is culturally conditioned ... [and] it may be necessary then to assert in the same breath that an official accepts gratuities but is not corrupt."[7]

In determining the level of corruption such an approach assigns a much more active role to the attitudes towards political and administrative behavior. A high degree of observed corruption may in such an approach reflect a high standard of ethics and a rigid application of rules rather than a high degree of real misbehavior. A cross–country comparison of levels of corruption would face difficulties since the underlying standards of ethics may not correspond between countries. However, some of the sources we included put a high emphasis on comparative judgments, i.e. an assessment of the level of corruption in one country is determined in comparison to the level of corruption in other countries. This forces respondents to use the same definition of corruption and to apply the same standard of ethics for various countries. This surely mitigates the bias that concerns Bayley.

Most sources focus on responses from businesspeople and risk analysts who are usually close enough to actual incidences of corruption and who can adequately recognize corruption when they see or experience it. Also some of these sources are sold to investors in an attempt to determine country risks. In this sense they can be regarded the market's choice for an indicator of corruption, as has been argued by Ades and Di Tella (1996) and Mauro 1995 (p. 684). The perceptions gathered there can hence be assumed to be a valid assessment of real levels of corruption.

The Gallup International survey differs from the other sources in so far as the general public is surveyed, that is, people who sometimes may not have first hand experience with corruption and who may have limited capabilities in comparing levels of corruption between countries. The methodological skepticism this implies is not reflected in the results. The high correlation of this source with the other sources is particularly useful in endorsing our approach. Although the point of view provided there may refer to purely local standards of ethics, the results are so close to the other sources that we are tempted to conclude that the perception of what is regarded as corruption is more global than many thought it might be.

We included only data that have been produced in 1996 and 1997. The assessment does not necessarily refer to the same period of time with respect to the real level of corruption. The perception by contributors may refer back to experiences made long before the assessment is contributed. In any case, the high correlation with older data indicates that corruption is usually not changing quickly. It therefore appears justifiable to regress the CPI also with older or more recent data.

THE RELIABILITY OF OUR DATA

Apart from the score of a particular country and its position in the TI-publication, the table given in the appendix 5.1 presents the numbers of surveys and the variance of the results. These data indicate the reliability of the respective score. The higher the number of scores and the lower the variance of the results, the more trustworthy is the outcome for a particular country. The high variance of, for example, South Africa of 3.08 implies that 66% of the scores range between 3.20 and 6.70.[8] Likewise 95% of the scores range between 1.45 and 8.45. Apparently, the average score is only to a very limited degree an assessment of the observed degree of corruption. On the contrary, the low variance of Thailand indicates that 95% of the scores range between 2.30 and 3.80. There seems to be a coherent impression of the degree of corruption in Thailand.

Deviating scores can on the one hand be due to subjective difficulties of respondents in determining the adequate score, e.g. limitations on experience and comparative capacity. It can on the other hand also be due to objective difficulties: An assessment becomes difficult in countries where some institutions resist corruption while others are openly engaging in illegitimate practices. A high variance may in this respect also represent a heterogeneous state of affairs. The high variance of Belgium and South Korea is noteworthy. After a series of scandals they may represent insecurities in the process of reassessing these countries.[9] The high variance of Middle Eastern countries reflects the perception that usually wealth and political freedom are positively correlated with corruption. Since these indicators are highly opposed to each other in some countries in the Middle East this may provide difficulties in the assessment of the level of corruption.

Perceptions may vary randomly with those voicing them. An indicator as to whether perceptions refer to some real world phenomenon can be obtained however, if perceptions are consistently reproducing similar assessments. Therefore, an indicator of the overall performance of the CPI in measuring real levels of corruption can be drawn from the high correlation of the various sources. Table 5.1 reports the correlation–coefficients between the corruption scores from various sources.[10] The idea of combining these different sources into a single index further serves to strengthen the index with respect to reliability (Lancaster and Montinola, 1997). The reliability of each figure is strengthened by including only countries that have been included into 2 polls at the minimum. Errors inherent in a single survey may hence be balanced by the inclusion of at least another survey.

DATA PROCESSING

The World Competitiveness Yearbook (WCY) in 1996 and 1997 asked business executives to assess their country of residence. With a response rate of close to 25% they obtained more than 3000 replies for each of those

Table 5.1

CORRELATION–COEFFICIENTS BETWEEN THE CORRUPTION SCORES

Correlation–coefficient	World Compet. Yearbook 1997	World Compet. Yearbook 1996	Political Risk Services 1997	DRI/Mc-Graw Hill 1997	Internet Corruption Perception Index 1997	Polit.and Econ. Risk Consultancy 1997	Gallup International 1997
World Competitiveness Yearbook 1997	1.00						0.89
World Competitiveness Yearbook 1996	0.97	1.00					0.82
Political Risk Services 1997	0.73	0.74	1.00				0.76
DRI/Mc Graw Hill 1997	0.80	0.81	0.69	1.00			0.68
Internet Corruption Perception Index 1997	0.95	0.97	0.75	0.87	1.00		0.88
Political and Economic Risk Consultancy 1997	0.95	0.93	0.68	0.64	0.90	1.00	0.88
Gallup International 1997	0.89	0.82	0.76	0.68	0.88	0.88	1.00

years. In one part concerning the performance of the government respondents are asked to assess the extent of "Improper Practices (such as bribing and corruption)". The endpoints of the given scale from 1 to 10 are described as " ... prevail in the public sphere" and " ... do not prevail in the public sphere". From these data an average figure is determined.

In a similar fashion, the Political and Economic Risk Consultancy (PERC) in Hong Kong surveyed 280 expatriate business executives, asking "to what extent does corruption exist in the country in which you are posted in a way that detracts from the business environment for foreign companies". On a scale from 0 to 10 a zero is defined as a situation in which corruption does not exist, while a 10 represents a completely corrupt environment. In order to give respondents some reference point, also the extent of corruption in the home country had to be assessed. Some effort is undertaken by PERC to provide respondents with a definition of corruption, i.e. "corruption is defined as the need for a company to offer bribes or other improper inducements to bureaucrats, politicians or other government officials, either directly or through intermediaries, in order to secure officials approval or achieve some other specific goal".

The contributions by DRI/McGraw Hill and by the Political Risk Services do not refer to surveys but to an assessment made by their staff after in-depth country analysis and discussion. Surely, this process is somewhat less transparent to outsiders. The Gallup International data and the results from our internet survey will be described later in detail.

The TI–1996 index[11] was the starting point for assembling the CPI. Each of the 7 sources has been normalized to the same mean and standard deviation the respective subgroup of countries had in the 1996 index. Hence, the inclusion of a survey which only scores a subgroup of countries affects only the scores between those countries and not the performance of the subgroup in relation to other countries. Each of the seven sources has been assigned the same weight. According to the respective quality of the sources, this appeared plausible. However, there is no "objective" weight, which can be applied to the sources and a different weighting may be justified. With equal weights, the simple average has been calculated from the normalized data. Since taking the average changes the mean and variance of the data, the final results have again been normalized to the same mean and variance that the countries had in the 1996 index.

The data by the World Competitiveness Yearbook, the Political and Economic Risk Consultancy and the Political Risk Service required no further treatment apart from the standardization. The data by DRI/McGraw-Hill required a (monotonous) linearization before inclusion, since regressing the data with the TI–1996 index yielded heteroskedasticity. A second order polynomial has been fitted with the help of regression analysis. The Gallup International data and our own survey require a more elaborated description since these data are for the first time presented here.

The Gallup International Survey

The Gallup International data is about the most interesting contribution to the index. An average of 800 representatives of the general public have been interviewed in each of a total of 44 countries either face to face or via telephone. These interviews were conducted between April and May 1997.[12] Question 5 of the "global" part of the questionnaire is as follows:

> "From the following groups of people, can you tell me for each of them, if there are a lot of cases of corruption given, many cases of corruption, few cases or no cases of corruption at all."

The groups listed afterwards are "politicians", "trade unionists", "public officials", "policemen", "businessmen", "judges", "ordinary citizens", "clergy/priests" and "journalists". For each country the numbers of replies to the 5 categories, "A lot", "Many", "Few", "None" and "No Answer", are aggregated, yielding categorical data. We made use only of the data for the 4 groups "politicians", "public officials", "policemen" and "judges" for reasons to be explained later. The 5 categories for 4 groups of people add up to 20 columns in a table. An easy way to present the data is by jointly applying correspondence analysis to these data and presenting them as in the Exhibit 5.1.[13]

A complete presentation of the data would require a multidimensional diagram.[14] Since we cannot easily imagine points in such a space it becomes necessary to reduce the dimensionality, which brings about a certain loss of information. The idea is that all points do not fill this multidimensional space equally but lie approximately in a lower dimensional subspace. This subspace has two dimensions here and is determined so that the loss of information is as low as possible.[15] All points in the multidimensional space are then orthogonally projected onto this plane. Axis 1 accounts for 53.8% of the total information and axis 2 for another 13.6%. Therefore 67.4% of the raw data are presented in the map. The 20 categories refer to Policemen (M), Public Officials (O), Politicians (P) and Judges (J) and "A lot" (3), "Many" (2), "Few" (1), "None" (0) and "No Answer" (N). Each of the 20 points can be regarded as the vertices of a multidimensional space, projected onto a plane. The distance between any two points now reflects how far respondents differentiate between these characteristics. This allows us to draw the following conclusions:

Exhibit 5.1

CORRESPONDANCE BETWEEN GROUP SCORES

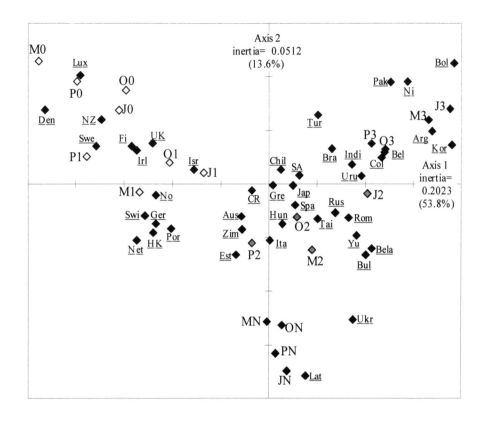

- Axis 1 can be interpreted as measuring the overall extent of perceived corruption among the 4 groups. While the categories "3" all cluster on the right hand side and categories "2" are also mainly on the right, categories "1" and even more "0" are further to the left. Since axis 1 accounts for 53.8% of the information we can conclude that the assessment of the overall level of corruption within a country is the dominant piece of information that is provided in the Gallup International data.

- The respondents can on average distinguish best between categories "1" and "2", where the distances for each group are highest. Low distances are obtained between categories "0" and "1". This is particularly noteworthy for politicians, where "P0" is hardly further to the left than "P1". One may conclude from this that respondents consider it of lesser importance for the overall level of corruption whether none or a few politicians are considered corrupt.

- Axis 2 contains another 13.6% of the overall information. On this axis the extreme categories "0" and "3" are on top, categories "1" and "2" further below while "No Answer" is on the bottom. The same average score for a country can be obtained by either a mixture of "0" and "3" or by "1" and "2". Apparently, in the first case there is more dissent among respondents. In this case, a country is located higher on axis 2, where it is closer to categories "0" and "3". Therefore this axis reflects some kind of variance of the replies with *dissent* on the top and *consent* on the bottom of the axis. Furthermore the category "No Answer" is on the bottom, proposing some kind of substitutability between "No Answer" and the more average replies "1" and "2".

- It is sometimes argued that different kinds of corruption might be more important to empirical analysis than the overall extent. The Gallup International data provide assessments for 4 groups of actors, which may allow to differentiate between kinds of corruption: For example, a differentiation between political and administrative corruption might be derived from this. However, the data do not reveal valuable insights in this respect. The groups "M", "O", "P" and "J" are assessed in a similar fashion since for each of the categories 0, 1, 2 and 3 the points are close together (e.g., "O0" is close to "J0"). This reflects that the results for the 4 groups are highly correlated with each other.[16] There is not much sense in constructing a separate indicator of the kind of corruption from these data. This reassures the validity of the CPI in assessing only an overall extent of corruption rather than focusing on different categories of corruption in detail. This is not to say that future attempts to distinguish between types of corruption cannot be fruitful for empirical analysis.

The location of a country within this map is determined as the average of the vertices (that is, the categories "P0", ..., "J3"), weighted with the number of replies each alternative has obtained. However, in order to make the map easier to read the results for the countries are given in principal coordinates, that is, they are zoomed. A country's position on axis 1 now determines the value that is included into our CPI. From axis 1 we derive the highest scores (most perceived corruption) for Bolivia, Korea, Argentina, Nigeria, Pakistan and Belgium and the lowest scores for Denmark, Luxembourg, Sweden and New Zealand. Other groups mentioned in the Gallup International survey (for example, ordinary citizens) have not been considered in the CPI since they do not fit into our definition of corruption as the misuse of *public power* for private benefits.[17]

Internet Corruption Perception Index

Similar to the Gallup International data our own results conducted at Göttingen University via internet (Internet Corruption Perception Index) had to be analyzed with the help of correspondence analysis. Between January and June 1997 we collected 246 replies to a questionnaire. Internet users with interest in the topic of corruption have been asked to fill out an interactive questionnaire. The sample reflects the typical users of the internet and has a strong emphasis on the western hemisphere.[18] The justification to use this kind of source is manifold. On the one hand it allowed for the design of questions, which are directed towards cross-country assessments and towards generating the kind an index we had in mind. Furthermore, although the sample design is still unsatisfactory and will be further refined in the future, the high correlation with the existing sources justifies the use of this data. Internet users have been asked the following question:

> *"You enter a public office which is authorized to grant licenses and permits (e.g. the license to conduct business). After you waited for a long time you are expected to pay a bribe and are told that otherwise you will not receive the license.* According to your perception, in which countries may this (i.e. the asking for bribes by public officials) happen? On the other hand, where do you consider it to be unlikely?"

Three alternatives "often", "sometimes" and "rarely" are given thereafter, which are supposed to be filled with country names. On average 7.5 countries have been named by each respondent. From this we can construct a frequency table and determine the percentage of "often", "sometimes" and "rarely" counts in relation to the total times a country has been mentioned. If we include only countries, which have at least been mentioned by 5 respondents, we obtain data for 71 countries. This is illustrated in Exhibit 5.2.[19] Since the frequencies of the three categories "often" (3), "sometimes" (2) and "rarely" (1) for each country add up to 100%, the three dimensions reduce to two and the figure presents the complete information of the raw data. As can be seen, the inertia is very high. This is also reflected by the fact that some countries were mentioned only as belonging to category "1" while others were mentioned only in "3". Axis 1 represents the overall extent of corruption since category "1" is on the left whereas "3" is on the right hand side of the graphics. On this axis category "2" is relatively close to "3", indicating that the respondents differentiated less between these two categories than between categories "1" and "2". The countries perceived to be highly corrupt now appear on the right hand side and countries mentioned to be clean on the left hand side. A country's position on axis 1 determines the score that is included into our CPI. Axis 2 still presents 28.4% of the total information. It can be interpreted as the variance, which is associated with the assessment of countries. A similar assessment of the overall extent of corruption can be obtained by a mixture of categories "1" and "3" or by a more frequent mentioning of "2". Although the same average score is obtained in these cases, the first alternative points to more dissent about the proper assessment. Noteworthy for this are Belgium, South Africa, South Korea and Cuba, which have a higher position on axis 2 as compared to other countries with similar overall levels of corruption. It is noteworthy that Belgium, South Africa and South Korea, also obtained a very high variance in the TI–index. There seems to be a repeated problem of assigning the appropriate value to these countries.

CONCLUSIONS

The design of a reliable and valid database for the levels of corruption has been proposed as a patchwork of very different approaches. Such a patchwork naturally contains disadvantages over a unified approach: Since each source has been produced for a different purpose, it usually applies a different methodology. This raises questions of comparability. While the World Competitiveness Yearbook might be the most valuable, it has the disadvantage that each respondent assesses only his or her home country. This raises questions as to whether the same definitions of corruption are applied for various countries. This problem is similar in the set of data by the Political and Economic Risk Consultancy and even more pronounced in

Exhibit 5.2

FREQUENCY OF MENTION OF COUNTRIES

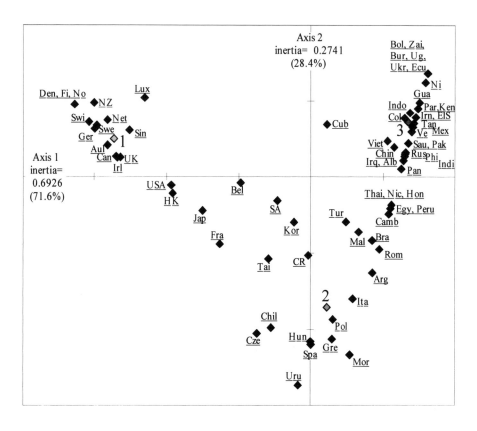

the case of the Gallup International data. A more global perspective with a presumably more unified definition of corruption is given by the two assessments of the Political Risk Services and DRI/McGraw-Hill. However, the precise knowledge about corruption might be limited there, owing to the huge set of countries they are assessing. This disadvantage is surely less pronounced in case of the surveys. These assessments therefore risk substituting corruption by other socioeconomic data which may bias their perception of corruption. For example, they correlate higher with income (as measured by GDP/Head) as the other sources. Last but not least, our own survey adequately asks for comparative assessments and overcomes the disadvantages inherent in the other studies but has an unsatisfactory sample design.

The very critical aspects of our data are however by far offset by the fact, that all the different sources are so highly correlated with each other and provide a very coherent viewpoint towards corruption. Although a unified survey which poses the right cross–country comparative questions to the right sample of experts from a well determined selection of countries and thus covers a large amount of nations would definitely provide even more validity to our results, it has to be stressed that the multi–method approach we have followed has a lot of advantages too: The fact that repeatedly similar assessments are generated by applying quite different methodologies serves as an indicator that behind the perceptions gathered is a good deal of truth.

NOTES

[1] In statistical terms, there appear to be problems of heteroskedasticity in the Mauro regressions. Also the scatter plots in Brunetti, Kisunko and Weder (1997) suggest that heteroskedasticity may be prevalent in the regressions.

[2] The R^2 is as low as 0.13, indicating that either too much noise is affecting this relationship or too little is known about other influencing factors.

[3] The authors suggest the index of public procurement of neighboring countries as an instrumental variable, arguing that industrial policy is justified by politicians by pointing to the behavior of their neighbors. Whatever a neighboring country might be in a scattered sample of 32 countries around the world, the level of corruption may show a similar pattern of regional spillovers and the exogeneity of the procurement–variable might therefore be questioned.

[4] The authors refer to a 1 point improvement in a corruption index by the Political Risk Service. This index has about half the standard deviation of the relevant sub-sample of countries in our index.

[5]   For an overview see Galtung (1997).

[6]   For a description of the Transparency International Corruption Perception Index 1995-1997 see Lambsdorff (1995, 1996, 1997).

[7]   Cited according to Lancaster and Montinola (1997).

[8]   This is computed by taking the square root of the variance and by adding and subtracting this value from the average score to obtain the upper and lower bound.

[9]   The high variance of lower scoring countries like Zaire is a side effect of the standardization of data.

[10]   The table slightly differs from the one in Lambsdorff (1995, 1996, 1997) since correlation values are determined for up to 101 countries and not the 52 countries of the TI-index.

[11]   See Lambsdorff (1995, 1996, 1997)

[12]   The countries included into the Gallup survey are Austria (Aus), Belgium (Bel), Denmark (Den), Finland (Fi), Germany (Ger), Greece (Gre), Ireland (Ire), Italy (Ita), Luxembourg (Lux), Netherlands (Net), Norway (No), Portugal (Por), Spain (Spa), Sweden (Swe), Switzerland (Swi), Turkey (Tur), United Kingdom (UK), Belarus (Bela), Bulgaria (Bul), Estonia (Est), Hungary (Hun), Latvia (Lat), Romania (Rom), Russia (Rus), Ukraine (Ukr), Yugoslavia (Yu), Argentina (Arg), Bolivia (Bol), Brazil (Bra), Chile (Chil), Colombia (Col), Costa Rica (CR), Uruguay (Uru), Israel (Isr), Hong Kong (HK), India (Indi), Japan (Jap), Korea (Kor), Pakistan (Pak), Taiwan (Tai), Nigeria (Ni), South Africa (SA), Zimbabwe (Zim), New Zealand (NZ).

[13]   The graphics has been developed with the software program SimCA by Michael Greenacre.

[14]   The total number of dimensions is 17 since the total number of replies are given by the replies to the first group and repeated thereafter for the other 3 groups. For Latvia no answers were given for "Judges" due to an omission in the questionnaire. Missing data are difficult to handle in correspondence analysis. We left out the category "No Answer" for judges, which would have been meaningless for Latvia. The variable is included only as a "supplementary variable" which does not influence the position of other points. In any case, for the TI corruption index a slightly more complicated analysis has been applied which used correspondence analysis separately for each of the groups with negligible differences to the results.

[15]   For a more elaborated description see Greenacre (1993).

[16]   Determining separate indicators for each of the four groups the correlation between them amounts to 0.85 on average.

[17]   Also, the results differed from the ones we obtained above: 1) Total inertia was much lower for these groups showing that the general public differentiated less in the

assessment of these groups. 2) Less information can be captured on the first axis which shows that the groups differ less with respect to the overall extent of corruption. 3) More information is captured by the second axis which indicates that the assessment of these groups is more divert.

[18] The replies come from people who are resident in the USA (101), Canada (20), UK (16), Mexico (16), Australia (11), Germany (7), Hong Kong (7), Indonesia (5), Argentina (4), Korea (4) and other countries (51). They originated from the USA (91), Mexico (15), Canada (14), UK (11), Australia (9), New Zealand (6), Malaysia (6), Germany (5), Argentina (5), Venezuela (5), India (5), South Korea (4) and other countries (62), while their occupation has been public administration (27), politics (27), business (73) and other (119).

[19] Notice the following abbreviations in addition to the ones mentioned before: Australia (Aul), Canada (Can), Singapore (Sin), France (Fra), Czech Republic (Cze), Morocco (Mor), Poland (Pol), Malaysia (Mal), Cambodia (Camb), Egypt (Egy), Thailand (Thai), Nicaragua (Nic), Honduras (Hon), Iraq (Irq), Albania (Alb), Panama (Pan), Philippines (Phi), China (Chin), Vietnam (Viet), Saudi Arabia (SAU), Venezuela (Ve), Mexico (Mex), Tanzania (Tan), Iran (Irn), El Salvador (ElS), Kenya (Ken), Paraguay (Par), Indonesia (Indo), Guatemala (Gua), Zaire (Zai), Ukraine (Ukr), Burma (Bur), Uganda (Ug), Ecuador (Ecu).

REFERENCES

Ades, A. and R. Di Tella. (1995). "Competition and Corruption." Draft Paper, Keble College, Oxford University.

_____. (1996). "The Causes and Consequences of Corruption: A Review of Recent Empirical Contributions." In: B. Harris–White and G. White (eds.), *Liberalization and the New Corruption*, Institute of Development Studies Bulletin, 27(2): 6-11.

_____. (1997). "National Champions and Corruption: Some Unpleasant Interventionist Arithmetic." *The Economic Journal* 107: 1023-1042.

Beck, P.J., M.W. Maher and A.E. Tschoegl. (1991). "The Impact of the Foreign Corrupt Practices Act on US Exports." *Managerial and Decision Economics* 12: 295–303.

Bayley, D.H. (1970). "The Effects of Corruption in a Developing Nation." In A.J. Heidenheimer (ed.), *Political Corruption: Readings in Comparative Analysis*, New York: Holt Reinehart.

Brunetti, A. G. Kisunko, and B. Weder. (1997). "Credibility of Rules and Economic Growth: Evidence from a World Wide Private Sector Survey." Background paper for the World Development Report 1997, Washington: The World Bank.

Evans, P.B. and J.E. Rauch. (1996). "Bureaucratic Structures and Economic Performance in Less Developed Countries." Mimoegraph, San Diego: University of California, San Diego.

Galtung, F. (1997). "The Social and Economic Implications of Corruption." In: *Transparency International (TI) Report 1997*, Berlin, pp. 76–78.

Greenacre, M. (1993). *Correspondence Analysis in Practice.* London: Academic Press.

Heidenheimer, A. J. (1996). "The Topography of Corruption: Explorations in a Comparative Perspective." *International Social Science Journal*, 158(3): 337–347.

Hines, J.R. (1995). "Forbidden Payment: Foreign Bribery and American Business after 1977." Washington D.C.: National Bureau of Economic Research Working Paper, no. 5266.

Kaufmann, D. (1997). "Economic Corruption: Some Facts." Paper presented at the 8th International Anti–Corruption Conference in Lima, Perú, September.

Knack, St. and P. Keefer (1995) "Institutions and Economic Performance: Cross–Country Tests Using Alternative Institutional Measures." *Economics and Politics* 7(3): 207–27.

Lambsdorff, J. Graf. (1995). "The TI Corruption Perception Index, 1995." Transparency International (TI) Report, Berlin, pp. 51–54.

_____.(1996). "The TI Corruption Perception Index, 1996." Transparency International (TI) Report, Berlin, pp. 61-66.

_____.(1997). "The TI Corruption Perception Index, 1997." Transparency International (TI) Report, Berlin.

_____. (1998). "An Empirical Investigation of Bribery in International Trade." *European Journal of Development Research*, 11(1): 40-59.

Lancaster T. and G. Montinola. (1997). "Toward a Methodology for the Comparative Study of Political Corruption." Forthcoming in *Crime, Law and Social Change,* special issue on "Corruption and Reform."

Mauro, Paolo. (1995). "Corruption and Growth," *Quarterly Journal of Economics*, 110(3): 681-712.

_____. (1997). "The Effects of Corruption on Growth, Investment, and Government Expenditure: A Cross–Country Analysis." In Kimberly Ann Elliot (ed.), *Corruption and the Global Economy*, Washington D.C.: Institute for International Economics, pp. 83–107.

Tanzi, V. and Davoodi, H. (1997). "Corruption, Public Investment, and Growth." IMF Working Paper WP/97/139.

Van Rijckeghem, C., and Beatrice Weder. (1997). "Corruption and the Role of Temptation: Do Low Wages in Civil Service Cause Corruption?" IMF Working Paper, WP/97/73.

Wedeman, A. (1996). "Looters, Rent–scrapers, and Dividend–collectors: The Political Economy of Corruption in Zaire, South Korea, and the Philippines." Paper presented at the 1996 annual meeting of the American Political Science Associations, San Francisco.

Wei, S. J. (1997). "How Taxing is Corruption on International Investors." Washington D.C.: NBER Working Paper 6030.

Wheeler, D. and A. Mody. (1992). "International Investment Location Decisions: The Case of U.S. Firms." *Journal of International Economics*, 33: 57–76.

Appendix 5.1

CORRUPTION PERCEPTION INDEX (CPI)

EXPLANTION OF THE TABLE

Transparency International Rank reflects the position of a country in comparison to all other countries that were included in the list published by Transparency International (TI), July 31 1997 (Lambsdorff 1997).

Score–1997 relates to perceptions of the degree of corruption as seen by businesspeople, risk analysts and the general public, and ranges between 10 (clean) and 0 (highly corrupt). Negative scores have been obtained due to the standardization process.

Number of surveys refers to the number of surveys that assessed a country's performance. Seven surveys were used and at least four surveys were required for a country to be included into the 1997 TI–index. Only in this case a rank is reported for a country. If two or three sources were available the reliability is lower and the country has not been included in the TI–Index

Variance indicates differences in the values of the sources: the greater the variance, the greater the differences of perceptions of a country among the sources.

Transparency International Rank	Country	Score In 1997	Number of surveys	Variance
	Albania	1.02	3	2.89
	Algeria	2.95	2	0.32
	Angola	2.57	2	1.13
42	Argentina	2.81	6	1.24
8	Australia	8.86	5	0.44
17	Austria	7.61	5	0.59
	Bahrain	2.84	2	0.50
	Bangladesh	1.80	2	0.68
	Belarus	2.38	2	1.15
26	Belgium	5.25	6	3.28
51	Bolivia	2.05	4	0.86
	Botswana	3.60	2	0.08

Appendix 5.1 (Continued)

CORRUPTION PERCEPTION INDEX (CPI)

36	Brazil	3.56	6	0.49
	Bulgaria	3.94	3	1.78
	Cameroon	2.27	2	2.11
5	Canada	9.10	5	0.27
23	Chile	6.05	6	0.51
41	China	2.88	6	0.82
50	Colombia	2.23	6	0.61
22	Costa Rica	6.45	4	1.73
	Cuba	3.45	3	0.46
	Cyprus	6.61	2	2.46
27	Czech Republic	5.20	5	0.22
1	Denmark	9.94	6	0.54
	Ecuador	3.41	3	3.07
	Egypt	1.94	3	0.57
	El Salvador	2.81	2	0.56
	Estonia	6.16	2	0.10
2	Finland	9.48	6	0.30
20	France	6.66	5	0.60
13	Germany	8.23	6	0.40
	Ghana	2.68	2	0.84
25	Greece	5.35	6	2.42
	Guatemala	3.87	2	5.04
	Honduras	1.98	2	1.10
8	Hong Kong	7.28	7	2.63
28	Hungary	5.18	6	1.66
	Iceland	9.65	3	0.16
45	India	2.75	7	0.23
46	Indonesia	2.72	6	0.18
	Iran	3.02	3	4.46
	Iraq	0.81	3	2.69
12	Ireland	8.28	6	1.53
15	Israel	7.97	5	0.12
30	Italy	5.03	6	2.07
	Ivory Coast	1.96	2	1.05

Appendix 5.1 (Continued)

CORRUPTION PERCEPTION INDEX (CPI)

21	Japan	6.57	7	1.09
	Jordan	4.29	2	2.89
	Kenya	2.30	3	0.89
	Kuwait	4.65	2	2.72
	Latvia	5.11	2	0.05
	Lebanon	0.53	2	4.18
	Libya	3.47	2	7.67
10	Luxembourg	8.61	4	1.13
32	Malaysia	5.01	6	0.50
47	Mexico	2.66	5	1.18
	Morocco	3.45	3	0.05
	Myanmar	0.76	3	2.14
6	Netherlands	9.03	6	0.23
4	New Zealand	9.23	6	0.58
	Nicaragua	4.19	2	3.36
52	Nigeria	1.76	4	0.16
7	Norway	8.92	6	0.51
	Oman	3.60	2	0.08
48	Pakistan	2.53	4	0.47
	Panama	1.70	3	0.48
	Paraguay	1.68	2	0.44
	Peru	2.90	3	0.17
40	Philippines	3.05	6	0.51
29	Poland	5.08	5	2.13
19	Portugal	6.97	5	1.02
	Qatar	3.68	2	10.67
37	Romania	3.44	4	0.07
49	Russia	2.27	6	0.87
	Saudi Arabia	2.64	3	2.17
9	Singapore	8.66	6	2.32
	Slovak Republic	3.65	2	0.12
33	South Africa	4.95	6	3.08
34	South Korea	4.29	7	2.76

Appendix 5.1 (Continued)

CORRUPTION PERCEPTION INDEX (CPI)

24	Spain	5.90	6	1.82
	Sri Lanka	4.17	2	3.46
3	Sweden	9.35	6	0.27
11	Switzerland	8.61	6	0.26
	Syria	3.73	2	5.93
31	Taiwan	5.02	7	0.76
	Tanzania	2.26	3	1.10
39	Thailand	3.06	6	0.14
	Tunisia	4.03	2	0.71
38	Turkey	3.21	6	1.21
	UA Emirates	3.35	2	8.06
	Uganda	1.67	3	0.16
	Ukraine	2.61	3	0.78
14	United Kingdom	8.22	6	1.43
35	Uruguay	4.14	4	0.63
16	USA	7.61	5	1.15
44	Venezuela	2.77	5	0.51
43	Vietnam	2.79	4	0.26
	Yugoslavia	3.46	2	0.01
	Zaire	-0.11	3	6.52
	Zambia	2.47	2	1.42
	Zimbabwe	3.77	3	4.64

Appendix 5.2

SOURCES AND ADJUSTMENTS

	Source	Year	Who was surveyed?	Viewpoint: internal versus external	Questions asked?	Adjustment process	# replies	# countries
1	World Competitiveness Yearbook, Institute for Management Development, Lausanne	1997	Survey of business executives in top and middle management	Assessing the situation of the own Country (internal)	Improper practices (such as bribing or corruption) in the public sphere	Original data normalized: adjusted to the same mean and standard deviation	> 3000	46
2		1996						
3	DRI/McGraw Hill Global Risk Service	1997	Assessment by staff	External	Losses & costs due to corruption	Second order polynomial (monotonously) fitted by regression analysis. Results normalized	–	106
4	Political & Economic Risk Consultancy, Hong Kong, Asian Intelligence Issue #482	1997	Survey of expatriate business executives	Assessing the situation in the foreign country compared to the respondent's home country (external)	Extent of corruption in the country and its influence on the business environment for foreign companies	Original data normalized	280	12 Asian countries

Appendix 5.2 (Continued)

SOURCES AND ADJUSTMENTS

5	Gallup International 50th Anniversary Survey	1997	General public (internal viewpoint)	Assessing the situation of the own country (internal)	A lot, many, few or no cases of corruption for the following groups of people: politicians, public officials, policeman and judges	Factor scores for categorical data determined by correspondence analysis. Results normalized	ca. 800 per country	44
6	Political Risk Services, East Syracuse, International Country Risk Guide	1997	Assessment by staff (Integers between 0 and 6)	External	Likeliness to demand special and illegal payments in high and low levels of government	Original data normalized	–	129
7	Internet Corruption Perception Index, Göttingen University	1997	Internet users	Providing perceptions of countries the respondent is Well acquainted with (external)	Are public officials often, sometimes or rarely asking for bribes?	Factor scores for categorical data determined by correspondence analysis. Results normalized	246	71

6

CORRUPTION AND THE BUDGET: PROBLEMS AND SOLUTIONS

VITO TANZI
International Monetary Fund

INSTRUMENTS AND EFFECTS OF CORRUPTION

Corruption affects and distorts what should be arms' length, or objective and unbiased, relationships between government officials and private sector individuals. Through the payment of bribes, some individuals succeed in getting favorable treatment in their economic activities from public officials. Such a treatment can either reduce the costs for the economic activities in which the individuals are engaged or it can create new opportunities for them that are not available to others. Acts of corruption may be initiated either by private individuals or by government officials. When it is the latter, they may offer favorable treatment in exchange for a bribe or some other favor. When this happens, corruption disrupts the competitive situation that exists in the market and may give a competitive advantage to some individuals or enterprises.

The literature on corruption has centered on a basic and, for some, a debatable assumption, namely that the more involved is the government in economic activity and decisions, the greater is the potential scope for corruption. This assumption is particularly realistic when the government's role is not played just through its spending and taxing activities but is carried out through the use of regulations, authorizations, and other quasi-fiscal activities.[1] In addition, the less transparent and clear are the laws and the regulations of a country, the greater is the discretion of government officials in interpreting and applying them. Furthermore, the lower is the relative wage of public employees, the greater is the potential for corruption. Thus, *clarity, discretion, and a reasonable wage* level are key factors in determining how much corruption there will be in a country (Tanzi 1995).

In theory at least, corruption could increase efficiency when the existing rules are too rigid and stifling and when the bribes to be paid to get around these rules are not excessive and are predictable. In such circumstances, the economic agents who want to get around the rigid rules know whom to contact to get the desired decision; they know the size of the bribe to be paid; and they have confidence that the bribed public official has the power and the incentive to comply with the term of the implicit agreement. In other words, the official will not renege on the promise and no other official will appear to put obstacles on the activities of those who have paid the bribe. Thus, the services that can be bought with a bribe are available to everyone and at similar and known prices.[2] In this case of (almost) transparent bribing, corruption may be less damaging to economic efficiency and growth as compared to cases where corruption is random and largely uncontrolled, such as it is reported to be in some former Soviet Union countries, including Russia. Some economists have viewed the former type of corruption as a kind of (almost) neutral tax that increases the cost of economic activity, but brings little distortion to the allocation of resources.

While there may be some truth to the above argument, its practical importance is exaggerated. It assumes that economic activity is damaged by the existence of unchanging rules so that the bypassing or the bending of these rules, obtained through the payment of bribes, removes obstacles to growth without doing any damage. Unfortunately, corruption is like a cancer, it starts in one specific area, perhaps the area where the rules are in fact too rigid, and spreads to other areas. In time, most activities and decisions become affected. When this happens, corruption becomes like a distortionary and arbitrary tax levied with uneven and random rates. It ceases to be "oil for the mechanism" and distorts economic decisions in ways that can be very damaging to the economy.

When regulations create the possibility of increasing incomes for some government officials, more regulations will be created or more government officials will become corrupt to get a piece of the action. Corruption may also affect the choices by public employees as to where to work within the government. There have been reports of countries where civil service applicants have not been guided, in their job applications, by the interest or even the wage paid in particular jobs, but by the under-the-table payments that can be obtained in particular positions. For example, in a South Asian country with high and increasing corruption, the number of applicants for well-paid foreign service jobs has fallen in recent years, while the number of applicants for less prestigious and less well-paid jobs in the tax administration has increased sharply.

While some of the more speculative literature of earlier years had hypothesized a positive connection between corruption and growth, recent empirical literature has pointed to a negative correlation. The reason why many economists now believe that corruption retards growth is because it affects economic variables that are assumed to promote growth. For example, Mauro (1995) has estimated the probable reduction in the growth rate that can be attributed to the negative impact of corruption on investment. Tanzi and Davoodi (1997) have assessed the impact of corruption on the size and productivity of public investment. However, corruption affects economic efficiency and, thus, growth in many indirect ways--some not quantifiable but still important. Unproductive investment may replace more productive investment even when the total is not changed; incompetent officials my replace more competent ones; public projects may be completed in a sloppy way, or they may never be completed; less efficient producers may drive out more efficient but honest ones; and so on.

Up to this point, the topic of corruption has been addressed in broad terms. The next two sections will focus more on corruption as it affects the public finances of a country, either through its impact on public revenue or on public spending. This is an aspect of particular importance that has not received the attention it deserves. The net *macroeconomic* effect of corruption on the public finances is almost surely to increase the fiscal deficit. The net *microeconomic* effect is the reduction in the efficiency of public spending and of the tax system. The effect of corruption on the public finances goes beyond the quantitative dimensions of its impact on the size of tax revenue and public expenditure that determine the fiscal deficit.

Corruption in the public finances reduces the ability for the government to pursue its basic public finance functions. It distorts the allocation, distribution, and stabilization roles of the government. The effect of corruption on allocation is obvious. In the public finance literature, the role of the government in the allocation of resources is justified in terms of the need for governmental action to correct for market failures. However, corruption distorts markets, because of the differential treatment that individuals receive when some of them bribe public officials while others do not. In some countries, corruption has led to the creation of monopolies when some individuals have been given exclusive rights to engage in particular activities. The "crony capitalism" of the Marcos regime in the Philippines created several such monopolies but the practice is not limited to the experience of that country.

The distributional role is distorted because those who benefit from corruption, and especially from high-level corruption, either as corruptors or as corrupted, are often better placed and better connected than those who do not. Corruption allows them to increase their real incomes. The stabilization role is made more difficult because corruption, and especially corruption in the public finances, tends to decrease government revenue and to increase government spending, thus contributing to larger fiscal deficits. Additionally, corruption obfuscates the relationship that exists between policy changes and the final results of those changes. For example, it should be possible to predict that a given change in a tax rate may result in a given change in tax revenue. When corruption is present it becomes difficult, if not impossible, to do so. And it becomes difficult to predict the impact of a change in public spending on a given social output.

CORRUPTION IN TAX AND CUSTOMS ADMINISTRATION[3]

Those who have worked on taxation in different countries have occasionally encountered cases where tax collection was much lower than estimated on the basis of available information on tax bases and tax rates. This difference reflects the known and common phenomenon of tax evasion (Tanzi and Shome 1993). Of course, some, or much, tax evasion occurs when taxpayers manipulate their accounts or their declarations to reduce their tax payment. This kind of tax evasion takes place whether corruption on the part of tax officials exists or not. However, some tax evasion exists *because* of corruption. This is the part that is of interest to us here.

Examples of corrupt practices undertaken by tax administration officials in return for bribes would include: (1) provision of certificates of exemption from tax to persons who would not otherwise qualify; (2) deletion or removal of a taxpayer's records from the tax administration's registration, filing and accounting systems; (3) provision of confidential tax return information to a taxpayer's business competitors; (4) creation of multiple false taxpayer identifications to facilitate tax fraud; (5) write-off of a tax debt without justifications; (6) closure of a tax audit without any adjustment being made or penalties being imposed for an evaded liability; (7) manipulation of audit selection; and so on.

Examples of corrupt practices undertaken by customs administration officials include: (1) facilitating the smuggling of goods across a national border to avoid tax and duty payments; (2) facilitating the avoidance or understatement of a tax or duty liability through acceptance of an undervaluation or misclassification of goods in the processing of a customs entry; (3) allowing goods that are held in a bonded warehouse to be released for consumption in the domestic market without payment of tax or duty; and (4) facilitating false tax and duty refund claims through certification of the export of goods that have been consumed in the domestic market or that have not been produced at all; and so on.

These are by no means exhaustive lists of corrupt practices in which tax and customs officials may engage. Indeed, where corrupt practices are widespread in a revenue administration, its officials are likely to be continually looking for new opportunities to engage in rent-seeking. In some countries, the highest bribes may be paid by a business man to a senior tax or customs official, for example, to secure a formal certificate of exemption from tax or duty. In the same countries, different businessmen may rely upon their personal contacts with low-level officials to secure similar results. In some countries, imports by relatives of the most senior political personalities have been given blanket exemptions, thus costing the country large amounts in foregone revenue and giving these importers an unfair competitive advantage.

Reductions in government revenue occur when corruption contaminates the tax and customs administrations, so that some of the payments made by taxpayers end up in the pockets of tax inspectors or customs officials rather than in the government treasury. In some countries, corruption in the tax and customs administrations became so pervasive that drastic measures had to be taken. In Peru and Uganda, the existing tax administrations were dismantled and were replaced by new institutions with new personnel, new salary structures, and new organizational arrangements. In these cases, an attempt was made to provide better incentives and higher salaries to the new employees.[4] In several other countries, the customs administrations were privatized by hiring the services of foreign companies which assumed control of the customs operations in exchange for a fee expressed as a share of customs revenue. Thus, incentives were introduced for the foreign companies to maximize customs revenue.

When there is corruption, the tax burden *as measured from the side of a taxpayer* who has paid a bribe to the tax or customs inspectors is higher, and in some cases much higher, than the burden *as measured from the side of the government*, which excludes the bribe. The difference may lead some unwary observers to recommend increases in tax rates, or the introduction of new taxes, on the assumption that the country is highly taxed. This difference in tax burdens may explain why the taxpayers of some countries complain about the heavy taxes they pay while the revenue statistics of those countries convey a different impression.

Many aspects of the tax systems may be affected by corruption. However, this phenomenon seems to be particularly significant in some areas. Prominent among these are the provision of tax incentives and the imposition of foreign trade taxes. Both of these areas have revealed major cases of corruption. In this connection, it is important to emphasize that we are not dealing with the question of tax evasion in general, that may or may not require the collusion, and thus, the corruption of officials of the tax or customs administrations. Rather, we are focussing especially on cases where tax revenue is lost *because* of corruption, and, thus, where there is an active participation by government officials. Tax evasion that does not involve the participation of corrupt officials does not fall in our area of concern. Total tax evasion in a country is often much higher than the tax evasion caused by corruption.

In the provision of tax incentives, some officials, either in the Ministry of Finance, or in other ministries (such as industry or trade), have considerable discretion over the decision on whether to grant or not to grant a tax incentive to an investor. The decision often depends on subjective considerations, such as whether the investment is "necessary," or is in the "national interest." Thus, some official has to decide whether the investment meets these often vague criteria. Often the request for tax exemption for some economic activity is made by foreign companies and involves decisions by senior political figures.

The value of the incentive to the requesting investor can be very high because it is the present value of the taxes that would be saved over the life of the project. One can visualize the situation in which an often poorly-paid public official has to make decisions that may be worth millions of dollars to the investor.[5] Furthermore, applications for tax incentives often require many contacts between the applicants and the officials so that there is ample time to develop close personal relations. In these situations, the offering of a bribe, often disguised as a gift, and the accepting of it are the likely outcomes.

Political or *high-level* corruption has also been linked to the use of tax incentives. High level political figures, including presidents and prime ministers or their relatives or close associates, are occasionally involved in their private lives in economic activities that can benefit from tax incentives. These political figures have the power to make, or to influence, the decisions granting the incentive. These decisions can save the investors, both domestic and foreign, much money at the cost of the country's revenue. The area of tax incentives is often linked with that of foreign trade taxes because the incentives concern not just income taxes, but foreign trade taxes and especially import duties. Getting an incentive that exempts an enterprise from taxes on imported inputs or imported products can save it much money.

Corruption affecting foreign trade taxes is an activity of both lower ranking officials and high-ranking political figures. When the latter are involved, the involvement is through close relatives or associates. Serious cases of corruption in customs have been reported in the past couple of years in Morocco, Argentina, Brazil and other countries. In Morocco, the head of the customs administration was jailed for major cases of smuggling. In Argentina, the existence of a parallel (to the official one) customs administration was reported. In Brazil, smuggling by navy personnel, using military ships, was uncovered.[6] In other countries, corruption has involved collusion in the faking of invoices to get rebates on non-existing exports. In some cases, as in Kenya, the magnitude of these claims became very large, thus affecting the macroeconomic situation of the country.

Many of the factors that may lead to significant corruption problems in the tax and customs administration are common to other areas of public administration. There are, however, some special factors that make the task of addressing corruption problems in tax and customs administration especially difficult. If the tax policy and legislation framework of a country is highly complex, as is normally the case with the provision of tax incentives, the taxpayers may often have to deal on a face-to-face basis with tax and customs officials to obtain explanations of how the laws apply to their particular transactions. At the same time, officials may have wide discretionary powers to determine such things as the appropriate tax rate, timing of a liability, tariff classification, or valuation to be applied to goods which are the subject of a transaction. Where such broad discretion is available to officials, opportunities for corruption are bound to arise.[7]

In poorly organized tax and customs administrations, complex, bureaucratic procedures can even make compliance with basic obligations to file returns, lodge declarations, and pay taxes and duties extremely difficult. If taxpayers have to complete multiple forms and obtain multiple authorizations to complete a transaction at a tax or customs administration office, it generally will require visits to a number of offices to get appropriate official certifications, stamps, and signatures. Where this occurs, opportunities for rent-seeking by officials will invariably arise.

Corrupt practices in tax and customs administration do great damage to the revenue collection capabilities of a country. On the one hand, there is the direct loss of revenue from each individual collusive arrangement between a taxpayer and a tax or customs official. But more importantly, the long-term result of all these individual actions by corrupt tax and customs officials is to destroy any notions that taxpayers can be expected to voluntarily comply with their obligations under the tax laws.

When corrupt behavior is commonplace among tax and customs officials, the incidence of taxation can become completely arbitrary. When a tax or customs administration's systems and procedures are weak, there is little likelihood that a taxpayer's noncompliance will be detected and appropriate sanctions imposed. When, in addition, corrupt officials are regularly helping taxpayers to circumvent their tax and duty liabilities, voluntary compliance with the tax laws will decline and so will revenue collections. If tax rates are raised to recover revenue lost through low levels of voluntary compliance, the result may be to increase the amount of the bribe that officials will ask to facilitate the evasion of some or all of that increased tax liability. Looked at in this way, corrupt practices in tax and customs administration might be seen as a major impediment to improving revenue performance in some countries.

If corruption problems in tax and customs administration are to be seriously addressed by a country, a commitment must be made at the highest political level to deal with these problems. If senior officials engage in corrupt behavior while embarking upon a campaign to eradicate similar behaviors at lower levels in a revenue administration, it is unlikely that such a campaign will succeed. Many of the measures required to build a modern professional tax or customs administration, where opportunities to engage in corrupt practices are minimized, are of an organizational and procedural nature. However, significant simplification of a tax system can lay the foundations for improvements in tax and customs administration that will reduce opportunities for corruption. A policy framework that provides for a limited number of taxes, with a limited number of rates, and minimum exemption provisions can make the tax system much easier to administer for tax and customs officials. At the same time, if the system is more transparent, its requirements will be more readily understood by taxpayers. If reform of the policy framework is accompanied by the introduction of effective penalty measures, this can provide a clear indication to taxpayers that their liabilities will be rigorously enforced in the future.

Simplification of tax declaration forms and filing and payment procedures can also reduce opportunities for day-to-day contacts between taxpayers and officials and thereby reduce opportunities for collusive behavior. Importantly, the introduction of simplified procedures can also significantly reduce a taxpayer's compliance costs and increase voluntary compliance.

The most important principle that stands behind the procedures and systems of modern tax and customs administrations is that of self-assessment (or self-declaration). This means that taxpayers are entitled to present to a tax or customs administration their returns or declarations setting out their calculation of tax liabilities based upon their understanding of the law. Of course, a tax and customs administration has the right to challenge and audit taxpayers' self-assessment of their liabilities on a selective basis. By reducing contacts between taxpayers and tax officials, self-assessment is likely to reduce tax evasion due to corruption of tax officials. At the same time, under some circumstances, it may increase tax evasion by the taxpayers acting on their own.

CORRUPTION IN PUBLIC SPENDING[8]

Corruption increases public spending and distorts its allocation. It increases public spending: by promoting unnecessary or unproductive expenditure; by contributing to the overpayment for some services or goods that the government buys; by making payments to individuals not entitled to these payments; and in many other ways.

To properly address corruption in public spending, it is particularly useful to distinguish between *political* or *high level* and *administrative* or *bureaucratic* corruption. Corrupt behavior that takes place during the budget *preparation* phase, a time when political decisions are made, reflects *political corruption*. Corrupt behavior and/or corrupt activities that take place during the budget *execution* phase reflect mostly *administrative corruption*.

Political corruption has particularly damaging effects on the allocation of resources because it tends to divert resources away from the function to which they would have been allocated in the absence of corruption. Two recent studies by Mauro (1997) and by Tanzi and Davoodi (1997) have attempted to show quantitatively the extent to which corruption changes the allocation of public spending. Of course, because corruption also reduces tax revenue, total public spending is also affected. Both of these studies use cross-sectional data and regression analysis.

Mauro's main results can be summarized as follows.

First, he does not find *any* relationship between corruption and the level of public spending.

Second, he does not find a *significant* relationship between corruption and public investment.

Third, he finds that government expenditure on education and health is negatively and *significantly* associated with higher levels of corruption.

Mauro's inconclusive finding about a correlation between corruption and the level of public spending may be due to the fact that while corruption tends to increase public spending out of available sources, it also decreases government revenue. Therefore, the pressure on higher spending is balanced in part by the reduction in resources necessary to finance spending.

Tanzi and Davoodi's main results are the following.

First, and in contrast with Mauro's findings, higher corruption tends to be associated with higher public investment *when the government revenue-GDP ratio is added to the equation.*

Second, high corruption tends to reduce government revenue, and, thus, it reduces the resources available to finance spending, including public investment.

Third, high corruption tends to reduce expenditure for operation and maintenance.

Fourth, high corruption tends to be associated with poor quality of infrastructure, thus reducing the economic value of the existing infrastructure and its contribution to output.

Thus, Tanzi and Davoodi results show that corruption can indeed have powerful effects on both the quantity and the quality of public investment. Their paper discusses in some details the factors that make public investment a particularly vulnerable area of political corruption.

Some of the major corruption scandals, such as those that shook Italy in recent years, have been connected with political corruption and public investment. The intellectual bias favoring capital spending, the controls that high level officials have on decisions concerning public projects, and the fact that in some way each investment project is unique and is subject to many kinds of designs, sizes, technology and other options, make public projects an area of public spending to be watched closely. The effects reported by both Mauro and by Tanzi and Davoodi have the consequences of reducing the rate of growth.

As is true of taxes in many cases, corruption in public spending is connected with bureaucratic rather than political actions. It is thus linked to budget *execution* rather than budget *formulation*. Budget execution involves several phases each providing different possibilities for corruption. During the *budget appropriation and spending authorization* phase there are various possibilities for *interventions* and *manipulations*. If the spending authorization is not granted regularly, spending units such as ministries will not be able to make commitments and, therefore, goods and services will not be delivered on schedule. The official in charge of issuing spending authorizations might favor a given ministry in order to allow that ministry to contract particular suppliers which compensate the official with under-the-table rewards.

In spite of the often specific nature of budget laws regulating commitments, the *commitment* phase of the expenditure process is a fertile ground for corrupt activities. The most frequent, and perhaps the most damaging of these activities, is the partial or total disregard of *procurement laws and procedures.* Regulations regarding prices, quality, quantity, as well as terms of delivery, can be disregarded in favor of particular suppliers who bribe corrupt officials. As the government is a major purchaser of goods and services, bending the rules in favor of a few suppliers can have serious effects on their competitors and thus favor individuals who are more efficient at bribing than at producing. Another possible case of corruption is the ordering of goods and services not authorized in the budget. Commitment of resources for goods and services not authorized in the budget often pre-empt commitment for some that are authorized.

The task of officials entrusted with the *receiving* and *verification* phase is to check if all the regulations have been respected. The budget laws of many countries prescribe that if at the receiving and verification phase, it is discovered that goods and services not conforming to specifications or not authorized in the budget have been ordered, commitments must be canceled. However, because of collusion among corrupt officials, verification procedures are not carried out and the existence of illegal commitments is often not discovered.

Corrupt behavior during the *preparation and issuance of payment orders* phase is essentially the same as during the preceding phases. It is based on the disregard of laws, rules, and regulations. If cash is not available for payment when goods and services are delivered, the government will incur arrears. Suppliers often accept arrears as a cost of doing business with the government. However, some suppliers will bribe officials in charge of issuing payment orders in order to get paid before the others. When, because of bribes, some suppliers are paid first and others much later, corruption can have a detrimental effect on those enterprises not willing to pay bribes, especially in periods of inflation or when interest rates are high. Those who pay bribes may recover their "investments in bribes" by increasing their prices or by delivering substandard goods.

In cases of severe cash shortages, when daily cash rationing must be imposed, the establishment of an order of priority among competing claims is essential. The official in charge of such decision has enormous discretionary powers, which can be used for corrupt purposes. By manipulating the allocation of cash resources for the purpose of favoring selected spending units the official can rearrange budget priorities for the year.

Corruption has often accompanied the establishment of extra-budgetary accounts. The very purpose of establishing extra-budgetary, earmarked funds and special accounts is to exempt some transactions from standard budgetary procedures and controls. While it should not be assumed automatically that these resources will be misappropriated, a lack of appropriate control procedure can create a fertile ground for corrupt behavior.

The literature on corruption has extensively discussed the consequences of the corrupt behavior of officials and has emphasized its illegal and criminal aspects. However, while these aspects are important, other dimensions of corrupt behavior are also important. We have already mentioned the impact of corruption on the size and composition of total expenditure, but there are other costs. The total economic and social effects of corrupt actions might be very costly and out of proportion to the bribes received by corrupt officials in terms of resources wasted, the opportunity cost of resources misused, and the inefficiencies introduced in the system. By diverting resources from their intended purposes, corrupt officials will change the allocation of resources as intended and approved in the budget. Thus, the decisions of the legislative body will be undermined and in the end the democratic process will be altered.

The next session discusses general steps that can reduce corruption.

Corruption in public spending would respond to the general actions against corruption. However, a few comments more specifically addressed to public spending may be appropriate at this point.

Political corruption and especially the one associated with budget formation rather than budget execution can only be controlled at the political level. Such control must depend on the existence of checks and balances, a powerful legislature, a vocal press, and an electorate that responds to accusations of incorrect practices. When the same political parties control both the executive and legislature and when the electorate can be manipulated, this kind of corruption can go on for many years as it did in Italy before Tangentopoli.

Bureaucratic corruption, at the budget execution state, is much more difficult to control because there are many areas where possibilities are open for corrupt bureaucrats to take advantage of particular situations. Apart from general factors such as the level of wages and penalties, the existence of effective administration controls is very important. These can be internal controls (i.e. internal to the particular ministries) as well as effective public expenditure management systems including clear budgetary classification, well working treasuries and so on.

STEPS TO REDUCE CORRUPTION

Corruption has moved from being a phenomenon of little interest to being one of major concern. Many now recognize that a country with much corruption cannot have a truly efficient economy or a truly democratic state. Corruption can be a cancer for both democracy and the market economy and if not checked it can eventually kill both.

Corruption is tied to many activities of the government. As we have seen in our discussion of corruption in the public finances, it can be carried out at the political level, by the leaders or the most senior officials of a country, or at the administrative level , by the bureaucracy. In this paper we have been concerned mostly with corruption as it affects government revenue and government spending. Both political and bureaucratic corruption play a role in the public finances. We have shown that it reduces government revenue while it tends to push for higher government spending, thus contributing to larger fiscal deficits. It also distorts the tax system and renders public spending less productive.

As with any other human action, corrupt behavior responds to incentives. Some incentives promote corruption, some discourage it.[9] Governments must address these issues more systematically than they have done so far. They must do so by looking at the transparency of existing laws and regulations, at the quantity of them, at the structure of government institutions, at the level of wages, at the professionalism of the civil service, at the penalty system for corrupt actions, and so on. In this process, the example provided by the leadership is very important. One should not expect to find an honest bureaucracy in an environment where political corruption is rampant.

Governments should not be fatalistic about corruption. With a well focused and determined effort, corruption can be reduced, although attempting to bring it to zero may not be an optimal policy. At some point, the social benefit from reducing corruption further would not justify the pecuniary and social costs of doing so. For example, it may require excessively high public sector wages or major legal or organizational changes. The optimal theoretical level would be reached where the marginal social cost of reducing it further would be equal to the marginal social benefit from the reduction. This level is likely to be higher than zero. In many countries corruption is well above the "optimal" level so that there is ample justification to try to reduce it.

The war against corruption must be fought on at least four fronts: (1) commitments by the country leadership; (2) reductions of the demand for corruption by the private sector; (3) reduction of the supply of corruption by the public sector officials; and, finally, (4) increasing controls and penalties for acts of corruption.

Commitment by the Leadership

The war against corruption must start with an explicit commitment by the leadership of the country (president, prime minister) that it wants a clean government and is willing to pay the price to achieve it. To be believable, this commitment must be accompanied by visible action. Leaders should not only declare that they are against corruption, but they should be seen as not tolerating any form of corruption, whether it involves family members, political associates, or other members of government. They must be particularly vigilant and strict especially vis-a-vis those closest to them who use their positions as gatekeepers to the leaders to extract rents from the private sector.

In some countries, political leaders have not been considered personally corrupt, or , at least, no acts of corruption have been traced to them, but they have, at times, tolerated, (or at least have closed their eyes to) questionable practices by family members, political allies, and members of their government. These sins of omission are as important in creating perceptions as sins of commission. The fight against corruption requires that neither of these sins be committed.

Reducing the Demand for Corruption

Corruption exists mainly because government officials find themselves in positions from which, through their decisions, they can influence significantly the activities of some individuals. As a consequence, particular individuals, such as investors, businessmen, importers, taxpayers or even plain citizens, can benefit from a decision that is favorable to them. In countries where governmental intervention in the economy is carried out mainly through broad, general and indirect policy tools, there is much less scope for corruption. Unfortunately, in many countries, governmental intervention in the economy transcends the use of general policy tools, and is carried out through regulations, authorizations, tax incentives, special access to credit or foreign exchange, and other tools that require direct contacts between specific individuals and public officials and require decisions by public officials which are tailored for specific individuals or enterprises. Such intervention creates a strong demand for acts of corruption.

An important reason why corruption seems to be more prevalent in developing and transition economies than in industrial countries is that in the former the role of the state is carried out substantially more through the use of rules and regulations and less through spending and taxing. As countries become richer and acquire the ability to raise the level of taxation and as markets develop more fully, the role of the state comes to be played more through taxing and spending and less through regulations.[10] When, however, individuals are required to obtain permits or authorizations (and often from several or even many different offices) to import, obtain foreign exchange, borrow, export, invest, benefit from tax incentives, open a shop, keep the shop open, start a new activity, and so on, it is inevitable that somewhere along the line bribes will be offered (or asked) to get the desired decisions. A bribe may provide a license denied to others; or it may provide a license more speedily; or it may reduce the cost of complying with existing regulations (as for example those related to health standards), or it may provide a tax incentive or subsidized credit and foreign exchange.

Thus, the fight against corruption must start with the pruning of the regulatory framework, at both the national and the local level, to eliminate redundant or unnecessary regulations. This exercise may also reveal that some needed regulations are not in place. The fight must continue with an attempt to make the regulations that are retained clear and more transparent to reduce the possibility of conflicting interpretations. Also, if possible, strict time limits must be set by which a given request must be accepted or rejected in order to reduce the chance that public officials may invite bribes by simply sitting on requests. The deregulation of economic activities which is characterizing the economic policy of many countries should in time lead to a reduction in the demand for acts of corruption.

Reducing the Supply of Corruption

The widespread involvement of the government in the economy, especially when carried out with non-neutral and non-general instruments, creates conditions which lead some individuals to want to bribe public officials. In other words, it increases the demand side of the corruption equation. However, as the saying goes, it takes two to tango. An act of corruption is much like tango because it usually involves two sides--one that offers a bribe and one that accepts its. It is conceivable that two countries could have the same instruments for governmental intervention, and thus the same demand for acts of corruption, but one might end up with much more corruption than the other. The reason might be that the willingness of the public officials to accept bribes could be very different. In this case, one reason for the difference might be the relative level of public sector wages and the status of a civil service job.

Countries that have low corruption tend to be those where the status of a civil service job is high and these jobs are relatively well paid. In this case, there is less pressure on the public employees to accept bribes (to make ends meet) and there is a higher opportunity cost to them associated with losing their government job. In some countries, however, public employees are paid so little that they are pushed, or even expected to get additional income, either by having second jobs or by compromising their integrity. In these countries, the low levels of wages are often also accompanied by little differentiation in salaries across the ranks which creates additional pressures for some employees and especially for those with more discretion on decisions.

Although the level of wages is far from being the only factor that determines the supply of acts of corruption, it is a very important one so that a country that sets the objective of reducing corruption must be willing to revise the salary structure for its public sector employees. Countries that over the years have made significant progress against corruption, such as Singapore and Hong Kong, compensate well their public sector employees. In Singapore, for example, ministers are among the best paid in the world. This indicates that the fight against corruption is not a costless one.

Increasing Controls and Penalties

So far we have discussed three lines of action in the war against corruption, namely the commitment by the leadership, reducing the demand for corrupt acts, and reducing the incentives on public officials to accept bribes. The fourth line of action must be related to the establishment of better controls and heavier penalties. The controls would be aimed at increasing the chance that a corrupt act will be discovered. The heavier penalties would make it more costly for those who engage in corruption to continue to do so. There is now an extensive literature that started with the work by Gary Becker that supports this approach, with respect to crime in general.

Countries could create the equivalent of a Corruption Investigation Bureau (as in Singapore and Hong Kong) that should be a high profile and politically independent unit staffed with well-paid and highly motivated personnel charged with investigating reports of corruption. This bureau should go after corrupt officials and also after those who attempt to bribe the officials. It should have the power to recommend adequate penalties (including dismissal) for those who are caught in acts of corruption. It is clear that the effectiveness of such a bureau will depend on its political independence, its integrity, its resources, and the extent to which its investigations bring effective punishment on those who are caught either as corruptor or as corrupted. In this context, the role for the judiciary is important. A criminal investigation bureau cannot be effective if its actions are not followed by the institutions who have the legal responsibility to punish those who commit crimes. Unfortunately, in many countries, the justice system has been undergoing major problems that have much reduced its effectiveness.

CONCLUDING REMARKS

In this chapter, we have discussed various issues related to the fascinating and important problem of corruption. We have discussed factors that create an environment where corruption becomes common, and we have outlined major steps to reduce corruption. It should be realized, however, that to some extent corruption is a reflection of society. Non-democratic societies, without a free press and an independent judiciary, are less likely to be relatively free of corruption. At the same time, we have evidence of democratic societies where corruption has been and is still a major problem. But all societies can do a lot to scale down the problem. The costs of *not* doing so are becoming progressively higher in a globalizing world. But the fight against corruption must be carried out on many fronts. There are no magic solutions for this problem.

ACKNOWLEDGEMENTS

The assistance received from John Crotty and the late Laszlo Garamfalvi on parts of this paper is much appreciated.

NOTES

[1]   Because the latter are more prevalent in developing countries, these countries tend to report higher indices of corruption.

[2]   At times, it has been claimed that the corruption that has existed in some fast growing countries of South East Asia reflects these characteristics.

[3]   Some of the issues discussed in this section are drawn from Crotty (1997).

[4]   For example, in Peru the salary structure of the new tax administration (Sunat) became the same as that prevailing in the central bank. Sunat has also discretion over a share of the revenue increase.

[5]   There is now some empirical evidence that supports the intuition that low public sector wages encourage acts of corruption. See Van Rijckeghem and Weder (1997).

[6]   Smuggling protected by corrupt officials is at times tied to the import of narcotics or even weapons. Customs officials on the border between Mexico and the United States have often been suspected of contributing to the smuggling of illicit drugs into the United States.

[7]   In these situations the interpersonal relationships mentioned by Tanzi (1995) come to acquire a particularly important note. In Morocco, for example, the average waiting period for clearing goods at customs is 16 days and requires 17 documents. By contrast, in Singapore the clearing of goods takes 2-3 hours and is mostly done by computers.

[8]   Some of the issues dealt with in this section are discussed in greater depth in Garamfalvi (1997) and in Tanzi and Davoodi (1997).

[9]   For an attempt to link incentives to corruption, see Chand and Moene (1997).

[10]   It should be recalled that some of the countries with the best indexes of corruption, that is those that are perceived to be least corrupt (Denmark, Sweden, Canada, Norway, etc.) have some of the highest levels of taxes and public spending.

REFERENCES

Chand, Sheetal K. and Karl O. Moene. (1997). "Controlling Fiscal Corruption." *IMF Working paper* WP/97/100.

Crotty, John. (1997). "Measures to Address Corruption Problems in Tax and Customs Administrations." Paper presented at The Eighth International Anti-Corruption Conference in Lima, Peru, September 7-11.

Garamfalvi, Laszlo. (1997). "Corruption in the Public Expenditure Management Process," paper presented at The Eighth International Anti-Corruption Conference in Lima, Peru, September 7-11.

Mauro, Paolo. (1995). "Corruption and Growth," *Quarterly Journal of Economics*, 110(3): 681-712.

_____. (1997). "The Effects of Corruption on Growth, Investment, and Government Expenditure: A Cross–Country Analysis." In Kimberly Ann Elliot (ed.), *Corruption and the Global Economy*, Washington D.C.: Institute for International Economics, pp. 83–107.

Tanzi, Vito, 1995, "Corruption, Government Activities, and Markets." In Gianluca Fiorentini and Sam Petzman (eds.), *The Economics of Organized Crime*, Cambridge: Cambridge University Press.

Tanzi, Vito and Partho Shome. (1993). "A Primer on Tax Evasion." *IMF Staff Papers*, 40(4): 807-828.

Tanzi, V. and Davoodi, H. (1997). "Corruption, Public Investment, and Growth," IMF Working Paper WP/97/139.

Ul Haque, Nadeem and Ratna Sashay. (1996). "Do Government Wage Cuts Close Budge Deficits? Costs of Corruption" *IMF Staff Papers*, 43(4): 754-778.

Van Rijckeghem and Beatrice Weder. (1997). "Corruption and the Role of Temptation: Do Low Wages in Civil Service Cause Corruption?" IMF Working Paper, WP/97/73.

7

RESEARCH ON CORRUPTION: CRITICAL EMPIRICAL ISSUES

DANIEL KAUFMANN
The World Bank

INTRODUCTION

Past research on corruption, both prolific and with a long history, covers many fields. It is not the intention of this chapter to faithfully survey where research stands today or to give an objective and comprehensive view of the many paths such research could take in the future.[1] Instead, I try to discuss areas of research emphasis for the next phase of corruption research in an admittedly selective fashion, explicitly recognizing the author's bias as an operationally-oriented research economist. As such this chapter aims at putting some heretofore under-emphasized issues at the forefront of discussion, as well as furthering debate on unresolved issues.[2]

Our central tenet is that advancing the empirics of corruption should be an explicit and key objective of action programs aimed at furthering in-depth diagnostics of corruption within countries and public institutions. Such an emphasis is critical to stimulate, sustain, and nourish, action programs.

Indeed, a complementary objective in the next stage of research in corruption is to translate such diagnostics and analysis of the empirical data into concrete policy options for anti-corruption programs. It may at first appear unrealistic to aim for such concrete and direct *operational* results from *research* in corruption, which some may argue is best left to "policy wonks" or to enforcement experts with long operational experience. Yet in the field of corruption, such view may amount nowadays to missing an important opportunity to advance rigorous knowledge on policy options.

This is because the field of "anti-corruption" action programs is at an infant stage, still populated by a number of myths and misconceptions in terms of strategies and policy implications. Such misconceptions are often due to the absence of in-depth analytical and empirical underpinnings of the proposed anti-corruption actions. The prevalence of advice to countries to mimic the Hong Kong Independent Commission Against Corruption (ICAC) is just one example. Conversely, many analytical papers on corruption close by mentioning generically in a perfunctory paragraph a "policy implication" – such as "caution" against rapid liberalization, exercising "care" in sequencing reforms, "tailoring" programs to country characteristics, etc.[3] Thus, a more explicit linkage between empirical research and practical and implementable policy actions in the field is called for.

Advances in the area of commercial trade as well as macro-economic stabilization policies may help place the state-of-the arts in terms of "what to do" about corruption in some perspective. From the late seventies to the late eighties there was a "revolution" in research and thinking about trade policy, essentially resulting in a practical consensus on the benefits of fairly liberalized trade regimes. With a few variations on details, consensus also took place during the eighties and early nineties regarding the benefits of rather austere macro-economic stances and stabilization policies, that is, on the key interplay between disciplined fiscal and monetary policies, a stable exchange rate regime and low inflation.[4] Research played a critical role in developing the consensus on policy advice, which has played an important role in economy-wide reforms throughout the world over the past dozen years. Moreover, it was often the academic researchers who played a pivotal role in promoting this new policy consensus.[5]

Appropriately phrased, the parallel applies: the state of the arts in terms of "what to do" about corruption is today where our understanding of policy options stood in macroeconomics and international trade about fifteen years ago. At such an incipient level the value added of vigorous research can be very large. Yet at the same time the parallel with the economic fields is far from airtight. In an important sense corruption is more complex and difficult to address. It is much more interdisciplinary in nature, it has long historical and political roots and a wide range of topics and issues are usually subsumed under the umbrella of "corruption."

DEFINING AND CIRCUMSCRIBING "CORRUPTION"

The disparate field of corruption spans many established fields. Within such diversity, the definitional aspects of what corruption encompasses have not been fully flushed out. First, this is because the conventional definition of "abuse of public office for private gain" can be subject to a variety of interpretations. In its broadest sense, it could cover basically any action by a public servant that ultimately will serve him or her to advance their own personal (or reference group) objectives. Somewhat more circumscribed would be to argue for "gross abuse", and "large" (or "significantly financial") private gains. Even then, each word in this conventional definition of corruption, namely "abuse", "public office", "private", and "gain", leaves significant room for interpretation. Thus, it is pertinent to raise a number of questions on this definitional issue.

a. How to interpret the various simple concepts adding to this complex definition of corruption, as raised above?

b. Would it be warranted to narrow or broaden such conventional definition of gross "abuse of public office for private gains"?

c. As a minimum, would it have to encompass bribery to "purchase" particular advantages from an official, fraud involving a politician or civil servant, theft, embezzlement and diversion of budgetary funds, patronage, illegal political and electoral funding?[6]

d. As a functional classification, what are the respective roles and usefulness of dissecting corruption into economic, administrative, bureaucratic, political, judicial or legal typologies?

e. How to incorporate, if at all, of issues of money laundering (including through sophisticated electronic technology), organized crime, "mafia", arms trade, drug trafficking, or nuclear smuggling into the discussion of corruption?

f. Should the focus be on corruption in the public sector (issues of theft, diversion of state assets and finances from the treasury), the interface between the public and private sectors (bribery and extortion), or within the private sector (fraud)?

The existing incentive structure for academic publication is not necessarily conducive to an in-depth rigorous exploration of the complex facets of corruption to help arrive at an analytically sound and full taxonomy. For a publishable academic article it is often preferred to circumscribe the focus to one rather narrow – and not necessarily crucial – dimension of corruption, and to probe such dimension theoretically in depth.[7] Instead, more operationally-oriented investigation of corruption through in-depth diagnostic surveys within countries are becoming the tool of choice in fine-tuning the definitional aspects of corruption and in groping towards a comprehensive taxonomy of all relevant corruption types. In a section below, we will present a taxonomy of corruption that has been developed at the World Bank to map relevant dimensions of corruption into various diagnostic tools.[8]

EFFECTS OF CORRUPTION ON ECONOMIC DEVELOPMENT

A priori it is uncontroversial to argue for further empirical research on the effects of corruption on development. We could frame the issue in terms of extremes: either corruption is seen as the *"cancer"* or *"scourge"* of developing economies, presaging *collapse* of their socio-economic fabric due to the extremely negative effects of such corruption (as often predicted for some countries in Africa or in the Former Soviet Union). Conversely, on the other side of the spectrum, one can view corruption as having some positive consequences, as in arguing that it is the *"grease"* that oils the wheels of development.[9]

In reality, however, empirical work illuminates sufficiently to suggest that neither extreme is likely to stand scrutiny. First, there is rarely a full collapse in a country since corruption is only one of the many important factors that explain a country's socio-economic developments. Second, corruption is often a symptom of more fundamental weaknesses of the state (see below), and as such it is misplaced to ascribe it the bulk of the independent negative effects of corruption on a country's performance.

On the other extreme of the spectrum, recent research also empirically challenges the "grease-the-wheels" view, which suggests beneficial effects of bribery in regulated environment. Empirical analysis, summarized in Exhibit 7.1, suggests that those firms frequently paying bribes end up spending more time with bureaucrats, not less, than those not bribing. The exhibit compares the frequency of bribery to the time that managers estimate they have to spend with bureaucrats in a country. Further analysis of these data suggests that those firms that bribe often tend to face higher cost of investment than those that do not, controlling for other country and firm characteristics (Gray and Kaufmann 1998).

In this context it is important to address *endogeneity* issues integrating, *inter alia,* arbitrariness and discretion into the bureaucrat's and politician's decision-making. The prevailing presumption in the academic literature that the level of regulations imposed on enterprise is exogenously given is simply not borne out by simple empirical observation. In practice politicians

Exhibit 7.1

TIME MANAGEMENT SPENT WITH BUREAUCRATS AND FREQUENCY OF BRIBERY

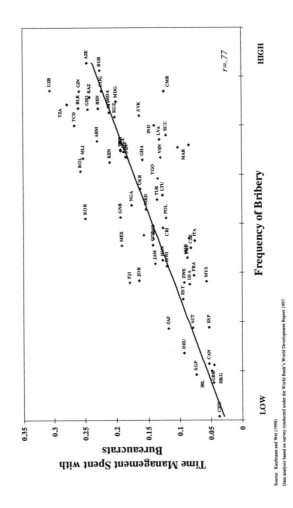

Source: Kaufmann and Wei (1998)

Data analysis based on survey conducted under the World Bank's World Development Report 1997.

and bureaucrats can adjust the level of intervention of the enterprise sector in general as well as tailor the degree of harassment to different firms depending on their characteristics. This allows for models where proclivity to bribe may fuel further regulatory harassment. This in turn theoretically backstops the empirical findings of a positive and significant relation between bribery and regulatory harassment (Kaufmann and Wei, 1998).

Overall, however, an empirical consensus is emerging on the detrimental effects of corruption on a host of development variables. Mauro (1997), Wei (1997), and the World Development Report 1997 (World Bank 1997) show empirically that corruption negatively affects economic growth, as well as domestic and foreign investment. These links are not established beyond doubt, since some of the statistical relationships remain rather fragile. This may well be a reflection of the less than ideal reliability in the measured corruption variable. The measurement of this variable is generally subjective and susceptible to a margin of error.[10] Further testing of these effects of corruption, utilizing a much broader set of available indices measuring corruption currently becoming available, may illuminate this aspect of the impact of corruption. This would also apply to the impact of corruption on public expenditures. Mauro (1997), as well as other IMF staff, for example, have suggested that there appears to be an inverse correlation between corruption on the one hand, and education expenditures, poverty, and income inequality on the other. These results, however, are not very robust statistically, and thus this line of empirical investigation is worth pursuing further. Additional research is also warranted expanding upon the important initial empirical tests in Tanzi and Davoodi (1997) suggesting that in corrupt countries the share of public expenditures tend to be larger, and the findings in Johnson et al (1988) suggesting that bribery is associated with a larger unofficial economy, in turn impairing public finances.[11]

In this context, it is important to incorporate the analytics and empirics of the *intervening* (or intermediate) links between corruption and development performance. This may lead to an improved understanding of the *indirect* impact of corruption on development, through crucial intervening variables such as distorted economic policy-making – as well as the results of vested financial interests that block progressive economic reforms, in turn impairing macroeconomic stability and openness of the economy.

So far, empirical studies on the effects of corruption on development variables have not rigorously distinguished between direct and indirect effects. Most often the corruption variable is introduced as a stand-alone right hand side variable in regression analysis explaining (left hand side) performance. Yet the study of development suggests that in the case of corruption the indirect effects may matter as much as the direct effects. Further, distinguishing between the two is important for policy and the design of strategies and action programs.

In fact, we need further in-depth analysis of the question of whether corruption is a *fundamental* determinant *per se*, explaining development performance, or a *proximate* cause for other, more fundamental aspects (where corruption is seen as "the other side of a weak state"). Clearly, in the anti-corruption agenda, the evolution currently taking place from the "advocacy-intensive" period to a more concrete implementation stage requires increasing recognition that there appear to be a number of basic, fundamental factors behind corruption.

Another area where potential value can be added is in setting up rigorous *counterfactuals* in researching key issues on corruption. This is particularly the case for in-depth country studies. Writing about "corruption being the resulting of privatization" as the soviet regime collapsed, say, in a Baltic country, ignores the counterfactual question of which corruption path these societies would have taken without privatization. In this context high returns may be derived from comparative research which pairs two countries that are similar in a number of respects, yet have taken diverging paths in terms of the possible factor(s) determining corruption. One such example would be contrasting Poland with Ukraine in terms of their different economic and institutional reform paths during the transition to explain differences in terms of corruption outcomes in these two countries.

COMPLEX CHARACTERISTICS OF CORRUPTION

What are the key *characteristics* of the corruption-vector which are relevant for understanding both its causes and its consequences? A number of dimensions are important, some of, which have received attention in, research, others much less so.

a. High versus low *incidence* of bribery or corruption. This is the most basic dimension of corruption. While many different empirical proxies purporting to capture the extent of corruption in a country now exist, significant further work is needed on how to measure and interpret corruption indices (see more below).

b. *Individualized* versus *systemic* (and *endemic*) corruption. This requires further understanding of what constitutes each type of corruption, and whether the causes and consequences of corruption themselves depend on what "stage" of corruption the country is at. Is it the case, for instance, that systemic or endemic corruption has a disproportionate (that is, significantly non-linear, whether higher or lower) negative impact on development as opposed to a much attenuated impact when there is an equal amount of total corruption (measured, for example, by the total volume of bribes in the economy) in the country but it is contained and individualized?

c. *Predictable* versus *unpredictable* corruption. Predictability is a term that has given rise to considerable research interest in recent years in a variety of issues and fields. In corruption work, a strand has emerged indicating that at least as important as the *level* of corruption itself is whether corruption is *predictable* or not. Our empirical research suggests, however, that the empirical relevance of predictability of the bribery transaction on a host of economic performance variables is not significant. The data appears to indicate in fact that the incidence of corruption matters more than the predictability of corruption. (Kaufmann and Zoido-Lobaton 1998).

Some notions of predictability may indeed be very important in explaining economic development outcomes; yet we find that dimensions of predictability other than of the bribery transaction itself (such as predictability of the regulatory, policy-making, and judiciary regimes) may matter significantly more.[12]

d. *Organized* (centralized) or *disorganized* (decentralized) corruption. This distinction was raised by Shleifer and Vishny (1994) and is closely related to the predictability issues raised under point c above.

e. Corruption which is akin to *"steady-state" predation* or *external shock-induced voracity.* The argument is that positive external shocks, such as oil price windfalls, may significantly alter the steady state of corruption, and induce "voracity" (Tornell and Lane 1998).

f. *History-dependent "lemon-reputation"* or *concurrent* (and factually based) corruption. The question here is whether there are major reputational costs emanating from historical corruption, which even after being addressed, significant reputational lags remain. Are there major reputational costs associated with corruption? Will a country that objectively reduces its level of corruption continue to be perceived as corrupt according to its past because corruption tends to have a "reputation"? Hence, will the country continue to be charged a risk premium based on its past record even when the reality has changed? Is the lead-time to correct public's perception longer in case of corruption than for other economic or social variables? Heretofore the work on this area has been of a theoretical nature. Empirical work may usefully be focussed on whether such reputational lags do exist, and whether they tend to persist for long periods of time. In case of the latter, policy options would emerge, since the informatics and empirical measurement "revolutions" underway should permit rapid and effective dissemination of indicators of improvement in transparency in a country.

Extrapolating from the intertemporal reputational challenge to a cross-sectional one, it may be useful to investigate whether countries tend to suffer from "contagion" effects in terms of corruption due to high incidence of corruption in neighboring countries, or in the region. For instance, Africa is often lumped together as a rather corrupt continent, when in reality there are some countries – such as Botswana – which exhibit one of the lowest degrees of bribery in the world.

g. *Asymmetry* in the *rise* and *decline* in corruption? Deterioration in the level of honesty within a country may take place more rapidly than an improvement; similarly, the longer corruption persists, the longer it may take for a given improvement to take place. Further, under certain circumstances, a significant improvement in corruption may take place only where bold reforms are implemented. The policy-based hypothesis is that incrementalism is unlikely to elicit results where corruption is entrenched. These hypotheses are important for country strategies, yet have not been studied empirically in depth.

h. *Grand* versus *petty* corruption: do they have a very different impact? While this is a rather basic question, its empirical investigation is hampered by the paucity of reliable comparative data on "grand" corruption. There is agreement that high level corruption exists in may countries, which not only involves large scale bribery among high officials (say, for large scale procurement in infrastructure and energy) but also includes embezzlement and theft of public resources and assets. Similarly, there is consensus on the negative impact that such high level corruption has. Less clear is whether the potentially pernicious effect of widespread petty corruption does have comparable negative implications.[13]

CAUSES OF CORRUPTION

A few salient issues deserving further empirical research into the determinants of corruption may be pointed out.

a. *Domestic* determinants of corruption in an emerging economy and the *relevant time frame* of possible interventions. We need to understand the relative impact of developmental-longer term and entrenched-institutional determinants of corruption versus medium term determinants arising from regulatory and/or economic policies and incentives. Further, what are the complementarities between various long, medium, or short-term determinants of corruption?

b. *Dynamics* of corruption within countries over time. How does a country become corrupt, and how can the process be reversed? Can vicious cycles be changed into virtuous cycles? Ongoing research comparing the evolution of former Soviet countries with Eastern European countries in the transition sheds light on this issue, and emphasizes the endogenous public finance nexus with rule of law, regulations, corruption and the unofficial economy. (Johnson, Kaufmann, and Zoido-Lobaton 1998; Newman 1998).

c. Why do *highly populated* countries appear to be *more likely* to be corrupt, ceteris paribus? Can further testing and controls validate this initial empirical result? And if so, what is the mechanism linking population size with extent of corruption in a country? To what extent the particular system of fiscal federalism appears to matter? Would the task of controlling corruption in large countries, therefore, imply different challenges and design than in smaller countries?

d. Can research provide insights into important *regional differences* in "fundamentals" causing corruption? Are there different "patterns" of corruption in Asia versus Latin America versus Africa versus Eastern and Central Europe?

e. *Foreign investor incentives*. What are the determinants of frontier corruption in emerging economies? What are the incentives and attitudes of OECD traders and investors to bribe in the emerging economies that they enter? Ongoing research on costs to business of bribing can motivate further policy and institutional initiatives based on the *benefits of collective action*.

f. What are the political roots behind corruption? Are certain types of political regimes less prone to cause systemic corruption? Preliminary analysis shown in Exhibit 7.2 challenges the idea that certain types of ideologies are more or less prone to corruption. The exhibit compares the levels of corruption in countries with the ideology of the regime – defined here as either left or right (Kaufmann and Sachs 1998).

Models of Government and Causes of Corruption

"Imported goods shall be sold in as many places as possible...[and] local merchants who bring in foreign goods by caravan or by water routes shall enjoy exemption from taxes, so that they can make a profit. The King shall protect trade routes from harassment by courtiers, state officials, thieves and frontier guards....[and] frontier officers shall make good what is lost.... Just as it is impossible not to taste the honey or the poison that finds itself at the tip of the tongue, so it is impossible for a government servant not to eat up at least a bit of the King's revenue.... And there are about forty ways of embezzlement by the government servant [enumerated below, for which commensurate penalties are also enumerated below]...

> From the treatise *The Arthashastra,* by Kautilya (the preceptor and King's adviser in ancient India), circa 400 B.C.

The citation from the age-old treatise by Kautilya attests to the ancient nature of corruption. More remarkable is its explicit acknowledgment and analysis of the problem, and the public policy advice it contains. Not only was corruption regarded as corrosive to the development of the state thousands of years ago, but specific measures were proposed to address it. The propensity of bureaucrats to be corrupted was explicitly acknowledged back then, and the link between illiberal trade, bureaucratic harassment at the border, and corruption was suggested. Further, Kautilya understood that corruption encompassed far more than bribery: theft of public revenues was explicitly addressed.

Unfortunately, in the intervening period these premises have not always been analyzed with such lucidity. Some recent writings even hold that liberalization and other economic reforms are conducive to more, not less, corruption. Yet there is still some clarity of thought in some quarters: a few months ago a senior official from the same country of Kautilya was asked why there was still so much bureaucratic red tape and need for "additional"

Exhibit 7.2

GOVERNMENT'S IDEOLOGY AND CORRUPTION

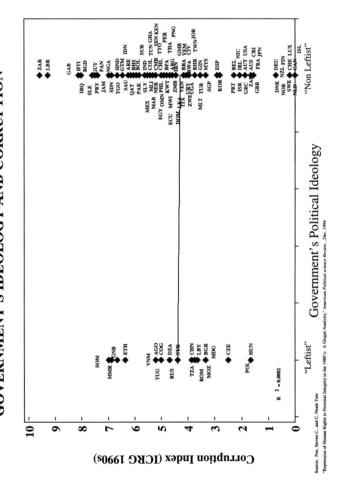

Source: Poe, Steven C. and C. Neale Tate
"Repression of Human Rights to Personal Integrity in the 1980's: A Glogal Analysis," *American Political science Review,*. Dec. 1994

payments - in spite of reforms. He answered that while the ongoing reforms had resulted in many of the prevailing *regulations* being eliminated, the problem was that that they had not eliminated the *regulators.*

One is then forced to pose the stark question: which model of government can be useful as a framework of the analysis for corruption? How can such a model of government help us understand what politicians and bureaucrats really do, and why do they do what they do?

For brevity, a simple characterization of the prevailing models of government in modern times has been i) the *helping hand* model of government, and, ii) the *invisible hand* model (Shleifer and Vishny 1998). Variants falling in between these two extremes have been advanced recently, such as iii) the *market-friendly* model of government, and iv) the *capable* model of government. The helping hand of government presumes that market failure is extensive, as are social externalities. Thus, in order to maximize social welfare, governments need to intervene extensively. There is an elaborate model of government associated with this framework, given its large and helpful role. At the other extreme, the invisible hand model presumes that markets functions well and that externalities are low (or can be internalized through market incentives). The invisible hand model has a very minimalist and specific role for government, such as the rule of law and some income redistribution or targeted poverty alleviation.

The models of government relied upon by those writing on economic development, whether in the academia or in the International Financial Institutions (IFI), have changed during the past few decades. During the seventies, following the famed McNamara Nairobi speech, the development strategy for countries like Tanzania, supported with large scale funding by the World Bank in collaboration with the Nordic countries, epitomized the "helping hand" model. At its extreme, the Soviet experiment was often justified within the confines of such view of government, which presumed a significant tendency for markets to fail and the ability of governments to correct those multiple and wide-ranging failures.

By the mid-eighties, as illustrated in the World Bank's *World Development Report 1987 on Trade* (The World Bank 1987), an invisible hand view was being put forward. By the early nineties the more "subtle" and balanced version of the role of governments as being "market-friendly" came about (The World Bank 1991). It gave governments a somewhat larger role than the minimalist invisible hand model had espoused - through concentrating on those functions which foster markets - yet its role was significantly more circumscribed than the older "helping hand" framework had been.

A refinement of that framework has now been put forth by the *World Development Report 1997* (The World Bank 1997). The emphasis in the late nineties is on a *capable* government (focusing more on quality than on "quantity" *per se*) where its role should be matched to its capabilities – a model that suggests different roles in different settings. Accordingly, this model also places itself between the extremes of the invisible and helping hand, as the "market-friendly" model did.

Not surprisingly, the invisible hand model does not have much of a theory of government. It can thus tell us little about what politicians do, which we need to understand in order to assess the nature, causes and consequences of all the abuses of public office constituting corruption. By contrast, the "helping hand" model (as well as the "market-friendly" and "capable hand" models) do have a theory of government. Yet all these models, which tend to be normative (rather than positivistic) in nature, are based on the premise that governments (and their politicians and bureaucrats) will maximize the population's social welfare. Thus they have difficulty in explaining what governments *really* do. More specifically, neither of these models tells us much that would be useful to explain corruption. The view that politicians and bureaucrats may be maximizing their own (or their narrow constituency's) well being cannot be easily integrated into these models.

The Grabbing Hand Model of Government

Enter the "grabbing hand" model.[14] In this political model of government, politicians and bureaucrats pursue their own, or at best of their constituent's, objectives, which are not necessarily consistent with social welfare optimality. The broader-based the constituency represented by these politicians, the greater the convergence of the politicians' objectives with social welfare objectives. Yet often such constituency can be much narrower (at an extreme, furthering the private well being of the politician himself).

What is the conduit for "grabbing"? The centrality of control rights entrusted by holding public or political office will be used to further the constituent's objectives (Grossman and Hart 1984). To pursue such objectives, politicians and bureaucrats have control rights over the economic life of citizens and firms. Corruption occurs when politicians or bureaucrats misuse or abuse control rights for private gain. We can expect, therefore, that corruption will be proportional to the i) extent of control rights by controlled by the politicians, ii) the degree of discretion and arbitrariness allowed in the application of these control rights, iii) the expected likelihood of detection and loss function (penalty as well as loss of government salary) associated with abuse, and iv) the professional and ethical values of the politicians.

Analytical Strands in Explaining Corruption with "Grabbing Hand"

The simple "grabbing hand" framework by politicians allows for the incorporation of the various analytical strands in the literature attempting to explain corruption. Scholars will naturally concentrate on their own field of study when explaining the causes of corruption. This can produce a rather diverse and disparate array of hypothesized causes of corruption. We attempt to utilize a simplified version of the control rights framework to depict a variety of these approaches and how they may differ. We can classify the approaches as follows.

a. *Political scientist* approach. Political polarization, lengthy term of the ruling party and leader in power, absence of political liberties and due electoral process and the like, would all be associated with accumulation of control rights and their discretionary application. These will, therefore, also be associated with an increase in corruption.

b. *Institutionalist* approach (such as in the New Institutional Economics literature). Institutional legacy of the past, in terms of norms governing accumulation of control rights and their application, as well as the historical ethical values governing the behavior of politicians and their institutions, would determine much of corruption today (that is, "path dependency.")

c. *Lawyer's* approach. The absence or weakness of enforcement institutions provides license to abuse control rights (and to further accumulate them). Weak rule of law, police, watchdog institutions and judiciary means a low probability of detection, apprehension, indictment, conviction and/or eventually serving time (or low likelihood of just losing all the ill-gotten gains if caught).

d. *Neoclassical economist* approach. High level interventions in the economy in trade and regulatory regimes lead to high level of control rights, which can be translated, into multiplicity of corrupt practices.

e. *Public finance* approach. Obscure and discretionary rules in drawing up and executing the budget provides arbitrary control rights to politicians and bureaucrats, who can engage in outright theft or diversion of public resources, provision of subsidies to favored enterprises in exchange for bribes, etc. Tax regimes characterized by high tax burden with discretionary rules and provision of exemptions are also associated with high and arbitrary control rights in the hands of politicians, which can be translated into profitable bribes.

f. *Civil service management* (or public sector management) approach. The very low salaries of civil servants, lack of meritocratic recruitment and promotion, and absence of professional training are the main culprits for corrupt practices in this view. It focuses more on the problem of the bureaucracy itself, and as such it is apolitical (or at least presumes some divorce form the incentives and behavior of politicians). In this view control rights are translated into private rent-seeking by ill paid, under-trained and unprofessional or demoralized bureaucrats.

g. *Sociologist* (and social activist) approach. Absence of civil liberties undermines societal scrutiny and checks and balances over politicians and bureaucrats, allowing the latter to accumulate and abuse control rights. In this view, the absence of active civil society (which *inter alia* includes a free press), and crucial information flows about control rights and their application (reporting on misappropriation of funds at the top, or how many bureaucratic impediments a firm faces when trying to get goods through customs, for instance), create the incentives for abuse.

EVIDENCE ON CAUSES OF CORRUPTION

While much has been written about corruption, both analytically and descriptively, the empirical field is at a considerably more incipient stage. This is particularly so with regard to analyzing empirically the *causes* of corruption (as opposed to the literature on the *consequences* of corruption, which is more substantial to date). Consequently, much of the evidence is still far from conclusive, and others reflect research-in-progress, requiring further validation and tests. Against such qualifier, however, it is fair to suggest that there is emerging empirical evidence suggesting that the majority of the *a priori* hypothesized determinants of corruption (as per the various strands of the literature summarized above) are important. The following is a brief list of the variables which, according to recent empirical research, appear to influence corruption (Ades and di Tella 1997, Kaufmann and Sachs 1998, The World Bank 1997).

a. *Political and civil liberties* variables. Interestingly, recent data suggests that civil liberties appear to be more strongly negatively associated with the extent of corruption than political liberties. This backstops the "sociologist/civil society" activist stance, and is consistent with the view that a participatory populace can place a significant constraint on the politician's ability to accumulate and arbitrarily use control rights. Further, there appears to be weak evidence that the length of ruling party or the leader in power may contribute to corruption.

b. *Rule of law.* The evidence points to a significant association between different rule of law variables and corruption worldwide. Variables such as protection of property rights, quality assessments of the rule of law, independence and fairness of the judiciary, ability to resolve commercial conflicts in court, ability to resolve dispute in government contracts in court, etc. are all associated with corruption. Given the way they are measured, some of these variables have elements, which are correlated and endogenous to corruption, and thus the direction of causality can not be unambiguously ascertained in the available studies.

c. *Public watchdog institutions.* There is a lack of rigorous analysis, whereby proper counterfactuals and controls are used, that assess whether governmental watchdog institutions have indeed been effective. Experts and consultants that focus on those institutions tend to suggest that they are effective by pointing out some country success stories where the watchdog institutions have had an impact. These writings fail to discuss in any depth the impact of the simultaneous broader reforms that took place. More analytical and empirical work is needed, however, to understand whether: i) watchdogs institutions arise concurrently at times when other more fundamental reforms are put in place, and while doing no harm they are neither necessary nor sufficient for reducing corruption;   ii) under what conditions these specialized public institutions may be counterproductive (such as abuse by predatory leader to prosecute the opposition); and iii) under what conditions it may instead be a very effective complement to broader reforms.

d. *Economic, public finance and regulatory environment.* Overall the evidence from research mentioned above, as well as our ongoing research suggests that high state ownership in the economy, excessive regulations and taxes over business, excessive arbitrariness in the application of such regulations, high black market exchange rate premia and trade restrictions, industrial policy protectionist interventions and anti-competition measures (including the degree of monopolization of economic structure in the country), and ineffective regulations in the financial sector and in the budgetary process are all associated with higher incidence of corruption in the country.

e. *Public sector management.* The degree of civil service professionalism, their training levels, as well as the professional practices of hiring and promotion appear to be associated with (lack of) corruption. More ambiguous is the evidence on civil service pay; the relationship is not very robust. There may be some non-linearities: there appears to be an association with lower corruption at government salaries that are multiple for comparative positions in the private sector. But at lower levels of that ratio the evidence is less compelling. The issue of whether civil service salaries are real "drivers" or mere "followers" of other reforms and improved public revenues is not yet fully resolved.

f. *General level of country development.* As expected, the level of income per capita or education, holding other factors constant, do explain some of the incidence of corruption in a country. Yet the alignment is far from watertight: Chile and Botswana appear to have a lesser incidence of bribery than countries in Southern Europe, for instance.

The above generic results, which synthesize international comparisons with data from anywhere between 25 to 80 countries ought to be regarded as indicative rather than definitive – given the state-of-the-arts of data gathering and empirical testing in this field. In interpreting these results, the problem of endogeneity should be kept in mind. Further, the above review does not account for the fact that there are significant regional and country variations in terms of the determinants of corruption.

MEASURING CORRUPTION:
IN-DEPTH CORRUPTION DIAGNOSTICS

A host of measurement and diagnostic questions deserve in-depth treatment in the emerging field of corruption empirics. In this chapter we raise some of these salient issues and provide some principles to consider when carrying out corruption diagnostics. The field is in its infancy; there are no definitive answers or fail-safe instructions at this juncture. Presentational brevity may give the misleading impression that some of the pointers below are more definitive than warranted. They are not. Instead they ought to be regarded as issues for further discussion.

Simply, the host of measurement questions can be organized around the basic questions of: *why* measure; *can we* measure; *what to* measure; *how to* measure and *who* measures; *whom to measure*, and, finally, *what to do with* the measures thus obtained.

Why Measure?

A one-liner suffices in answering at the more obvious level, since by now there is little debate and plenty of evidence on the ill-effects of corruption. What is often underplayed, however, is how insightful empirical measures of corruption can be for a host of institutional and governance analysis (too often long in prose and short on data). Corruption is, after all, a symptom of weakness of the state. As such, it is an empirical window to deeper underlying problems. Further, measuring corruption can be a powerful educational and activist tool for civil society and reformist officials in spearheading change.

Can We Really Measure?

Given the intrinsically secretive nature of corrupt activities, collecting reliable quantitative information is virtually impossible. Thus we need to rely on more abstract concepts, a few proxies, and anecdotal evidence (including the customary chat with the cab driver and after dinner drinks with local friends). This may be setting a "straw man", but the incorrect view just stated prevailed for a long time among many, and thus empirical measures and its analysis was scant at best. But in reality both the extent and nature of corruption can be measured and assessed with some degree of confidence. There is an emerging body of data on the incidence of bribery and corruption, covering about 100 countries; for over one-half that sample the data sources are multiple and cover a number of aspects of corruption.

What to Measure?

Let us use the conventional definition of corruption as "abuse of public office for private gain". *What to measure* would then lead us to consider different types of *abuses,* different types of *public offices*, some types of *private gains*, and *factors influencing* such abuses. Accordingly, we focus on typologies of corruption, agencies to look at, and certain financial transactions, before suggesting complementing direct corruption measures with proximates and possible causes of corruption.

Types of Abuses, or, a Typology of Corruption

The abuse of power can cover bribery (and extortion), theft, illegal political contributions, patronage, and illegal exercise of insider information. Bribery and extortion encompasses a payoff for a wide variety of illicit activities.

a. Getting around *licenses*, permits and signatures.

b. Acquiring *monopolistic* power (for example, through creation of entry barriers for competitors).

c. Access to public *goods,* including illegal award of public procurement contracts.

d. Access to the use of public *physical assets*, or their outright stripping and appropriation.

e. Access to preferential *financial assets* (credit).

f. *Illegal trade* in goods banned for security and health considerations, such as drugs and nuclear materials.

g. Illicit *financial transactions*, such as money laundering and illegal exercise by official of insider information for financial sector activities.

h. Influencing administrative or legislative actions, and,

i.   Influencing judicial decisions.

Often in typologies of corruption the monopolistic power category is omitted, yet it may be one of the most insidious forms given the huge rents and bribes involved in some sectors, such as in the case of energy and telecommunications in many countries. These mammoth monopolistic rents, in turn, can alter the balance of political power as well as how government is run and by whom.

In order to assess the damage from bribery, and to design policies, it is important to try and capture the distinction between two types of bribes. On the one hand, bribes may be paid in order to ignore *counterproductive* regulations, as is commonly the case with excessive regulations governing manufacturing and service enterprises. On the other hand, bribes may also be paid to get around *socially necessary* regulations, such as those regulating nuclear materials, protection of the natural environment, or sound banking systems. The outcomes and policy implications of each type are very different.

Theft covers misappropriation of public budgetary and foreign exchange flows, as well as appropriation of physical assets such as capital goods and real estate. Patronage covers preferential access to coveted jobs on the basis of undue personal influence of public official, and often is associated with a bribe or exchange of favors. While patronage is often regarded as a milder form of corruption than bribery or theft, when systemic it can have disastrous effects on socio-economic development, such as during the Soviet Union times - where a whole system of politicized economic and industrial activity was built around patronage.

Further, patronage often closely interacts with the other forms of corruption. In some of the former communist countries, for example, getting coveted ministerial positions now command multi-million dollar upfront "fees." These fees are payable by the supporters of the candidate presumably as investment for the expected regulations and public transactions that will benefit such backers during the minister's tenure. In some countries in other regions coveted positions are given to next of kin of the leader to safeguard continuous access to large share of the spoils. A detailed typology of corruption, along with its mapping to different diagnostic tools, is shown in Appendix 7.1.

The implementation of a diagnostic in a particular country does not have to include all the categories listed in the above typology. Prior to full implementation of a particular measurement approach existing information on the country would be gathered and reviewed, with a view to focus on the aspects of corruption, which *a priori* are most relevant. For instance, depending on the country particulars, attempting to measure insider trading or illegal political contributions may not be a priority relative to other forms of corruption. Conversely, however, it is imperative to focus on the selected "forms" of possible corruption in the country and attempt to measure them with some degree of specificity (as opposed to the common practice of asking very generic perception questions about the prevalence of corruption in the country). Value of such a focused measurement can be seen in some exhibits in Appendix 7.2. These exhibits identify the frequency of different types of corruption and the levels at which corruption tends to be high in Albania and Georgia.[15] Clearly such data would be of much more help in designing strategies to combat corruption than surveys that attempt to summarize corruption within a country with one index number.

Agency Focus

The operational objective for a diagnostic is to cover the key public sector agencies. In particular, data would be gathered on central government administration, some on local governments, customs and border crossings, state banks, post office, police, judiciary, ministries of finance, and trade, sectoral ministries, public health institutions, public services (water, gas, electricity), tax authorities, banking and insurance, housing and land authorities.

The selection of which agencies to cover, and particular approach to questions on the agencies will be driven by the institutional setup of the country, the typologies of corruption to be covered and the choice(s) of the unit of survey observation (section below).

Financial Transparency Focus

This focus would be particularly appropriate where the diagnostic need is a response to a narrower (and usually urgent) consideration than overall corruption in the country, focused in particular on the antecedents of a financial crisis. Currently it may be pertinent to have such narrow focus for the first stage of a review in some countries in East Asia undergoing such financial crises - where lack of financial transparency appear to be closely related to the resulting crisis. In such settings it would be appropriate to study the problems of lack of transparency and timely provision of information in the public budgetary accounts, as well as obscure accounting and misinformation on the actual balance of payments and indebtedness situation, and insider lending and lack of transparency in the accounts and activities of the major financial institutions (public and private, and particularly in the inter-linked public-private lending decisions).

In this context, complex (and difficult to document) forms of corruption may take place. In the case of some countries in East Asia, for example, influential domestic banks with significant foreign exchange exposures may have influenced the conduct of exchange rate policy through their inside relationships with influential politicians. Publicly available information on these exposures and the inside links may have influenced the conduct of the policy and might have averted the crisis.

Proximates, Correlates, and Fundamentals: Measuring Other Variables

The above sections discussed different forms of corruption, agencies and areas of focus that need to be measured. An in-depth assessment should go beyond covering directly the important aspects of corruption and should also gather information on proximates, correlates and fundamental factors potentially driving corruption. First, as stated above, corruption is a symptom, and is closely related to a host of other economic, institutional, and political variables. Gathering information on regulatory, financial, economic, governance and rule of law variables provides a more comprehensive assessment of corruption, and would be an input into the analysis of its main causes. Equally important is the gathering of information on potential consequences of corruption, since it is part of the broad governance picture and ultimately a key measure of impact for evaluation assessment. Further, some "consequences" of corruption, such as tax revenues and budgetary expenditures, also have a causal effect on the existence of corruption (through feedback loops).

How (and whom) to measure?

We discuss types of approaches to measurement, and then briefly assess their relative reliability.

Approaches to Measurement

We could classify them into the following categories.

a. *Surveying* particular "populations" on their experiences and perceptions. There are many types of surveys, and a key typology is by different units of observation.

 1. Asking firms (which could be a cross-country comparative survey or a more in-depth country specific survey – see, for instance, the table on "bribe fee" list in some countries in the FSU shown in Appendix 7.3.

 2. Asking public service users (service delivery surveys, rating a multiplicity of public service providers, such as those carried out by EDI of the World Bank and by a local NGO in Bangalore, India).

 3. Citizen polls of perceptions (e.g. Gallup).

 4. Narrowly focused user survey for single-agency diagnostic (such as importers for surveying customs; truck drivers for assessing road police and border guards, etc.), and,

 5. Asking public officials (here the challenge is to extract reliable information, which from our experience is best achieved when the officials are not in their offices, preferably during short-term training abroad or equivalent).

b. Asking experts. This is the approach to comparative data gathering used by commercial risk agencies, such as *International Country Risk Guide (ICRG), Standard and Poor-DRI,* and the *Economist Intelligence Unit.* The advantage of these types of surveys is that they have a continuous coverage over time, and about 100 countries are included. Yet only a few experts for each country are consulted and hence, there is a significant element of subjectivity.

c. Using existing *"composite poll of polls"*. This is the approach of the Transparency International's (TI) Corruption Perception Index[16] which combines the existing surveys, some based on responses by firms (e.g. WCS), some by experts (for example, International Country Risk Guide). Space limitation does not permit an evaluation of the advantages and disadvantages of this index, and of the key recommendations for improving upon the index from 1998 onwards. Yet in brief, the TI index for 1997 covered only 52 countries, was not strictly comparable across time, and country rankings for any particular year were subject to a significant margin of error.[17] Nonetheless, as a broadly indicative estimate of whether perceptions are that the country is very corrupt, relatively corrupt, somewhat corrupt, or relatively free of corruption the TI index has served as a useful "flag"(as well as raising awareness about corruption generally). For research purposes, however, this indicator needs to be treated with caution.[18]

d. Gathering existing *"hard"* *quantitative* data, sources for which would include the following.

1. Cost and price data on procurement and provision of homogenous public goods (such as cost of procuring generic aspirins for hospitals or school lunches) in all localities in the country.

2. Public investment and expenditure reviews, whose objective would be broader than corruption diagnostic, yet could provide a wealth of information. For the purpose of corruption diagnostics, information on "leakages," extra-budgetary accounts, white elephant projects, extent of ghost workers, civil servant salary structure and wage bill, etc. would be useful.

3. Balance of Payments (BOP) data to assess extent of capital flight, discrepancies between customs and BOP information, discrepancies between countries' officially recorded exports and recipient countries' information on imports from the country under study.

4. In-depth customs data analysis, including duty collections.

5. Tax collection data. Estimating degree of evasion of VAT or sales tax and corporate taxes is possible in most settings, and is closely correlated with bribery.

6. Jurimetric data measuring processing times within legal institutions to assess corruption in the judiciary.

7. Data on the extent and evolution of the unofficial economy in the country which we also find to be closely associated with the incidence of corruption in the country – and for which currently we are gathering a relatively comprehensive data set for about 75 countries.

e. Using in-depth *qualitative information*. This is an essential complement to the quantitative data discussed above. There is a need for an understanding of the various forms corruption takes and its causes in a country through in-depth interviews, as well as specific political, institutional, public sector management and legal analysis. Causes of corruption could include, for example, the role of the leadership, the degree of political fractionalization and ethnicity.

f.   *Procurement data* from International Financial Institutions and other donor-financed projects in the country. This is a potentially rich and often underestimated source of complementary information. Even simple indicators such as gross cost or time overruns in projects may raise a flag regarding possible malfeasance, warranting further review and data gathering at the project level. Further, given the extensive data bank for Bank projects it is possible to compare unit costs for standard items across space and time relatively easily. Wide discrepancies in these actual standard unit costs would be suggestive in an analysis of possible corruption.

g.   *Survey data on trends* over time. Some surveys have asked for the respondents' assessment of the trend in the incidence of corruption over the past three or five years. Combined with data on current level of incidence, and other hard data, this can be important. The diagnosis and policy actions for a given incidence level of corruption may be different when the trend has been improving versus where it has been deteriorating. In general, questions today from the same respondent about trends in the recent past may be superior to general perception index comparisons over a few years for indices that are measured annually. The latter can be used as a measure, but not from year to year (over 5 years, for instance, with moving averages if possible).

Reliability, Prioritization, and Integration of the Various Approaches

The menu of different approaches already outlined poses the challenge of focusing and choosing particular approaches, which as stated above will vary depending on country conditions and objectives. Furthermore, reliability of the particular empirical approach is important. Generally speaking, specific quantitative (e.g. bribe in dollars, or as a percent "cut" in procurement cost) answers on bribery and corruption (by types), from a relatively large number of respondents, would rate highly. At the other extreme of the spectrum, general perception answers on societal corruption by an "expert" or a few citizens (in a scale of, say, 1 to 5) would be less useful. In between one finds the gamut of approach to survey questions that may be somewhat less general, somewhat more specific to the own experience of the respondent (or her reference group), and a tad less subjective.

These tradeoffs cannot, of course, be avoided. Usually the more detailed and useful the specific information gathered, the more expensive and time consuming it would have been to gather it in the first place. A firm-level survey which requests monetary information of different types of payoffs, for instance, require skilled face-to-face interviewer skills, time and patience (and often repeated visits), and special questionnaire design. Furthermore, pilots may be necessary and the survey instrument usually will be long since it cannot work as a stand-alone brief "corruption" survey questionnaire.

The budgetary constraints governing these diagnostics suggest the importance to be attached to deciding on an optimal mix of data gathering instruments - which, while multi-pronged (rather than relying on a single survey or data source), will be very much a subset of the long list above. In terms of steps, it is recommended to first do an inventory on the available information and surveys on the country. This, complemented by the information by the staff working on the country, and indications on the interest and commitment by different stakeholders in the client country itself, will provide an initial prior on what areas to focus the diagnostic, and where the empirical gaps requiring further data gathering remain.

What to do with Measures

Two exhibits perhaps best summarize our preliminary understanding of how best to use information that has been collected through corruption diagnostics. Exhibit 7.3 shows how we can move from information and data collected at the global as well as the local levels to carry out analysis at various levels and finally to convince partners in a coalition of interested parties whose cooperation will be essential for a successful fight against corruption. The exhibit shows how data on corruption and empirical analysis can provide input for analysis for different groups of interested parties. Exhibit 7.4 shows how we can graduate from vague levels of analysis, thinking, and commitments to specific approaches and "frames-of-mind" that will address practical and implementable issues.

Exhibit 7.3

NEW EMPIRICAL FRONTIERS IN ANTI-CORRUPTION: DIAGNOSTICS AND ACTION PROGRAMS

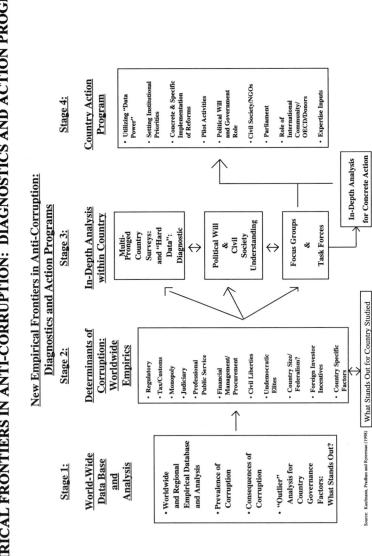

New Empirical Frontiers in Anti-Corruption:
Diagnostics and Action Programs

Stage 1:

World-Wide Data Base and Analysis

- Worldwide and Regional Empirical Database and Analysis
- Prevalence of Corruption
- Consequences of Corruption
- "Outlier" Analysis for Country Governance Factors: What Stands Out?

Stage 2:

Determinants of Corruption: Worldwide Empirics

- Regulatory
- Tax/Customs
- Monopoly
- Judiciary
- Professional Public Service
- Financial Management/ Procurement
- Civil Liberties
- Undemocratic Elites
- Country Size/ Federalism?
- Foreign Investor Incentives
- Country Specific Factors

What Stands Out for Country Studied

Stage 3:

In-Depth Analysis within Country

Multi-Pronged Country Surveys: and "Hard Data": Diagnostic

Political Will & Civil Society Understanding

Focus Groups & Task Forces

In-Depth Analysis for Concrete Action

Stage 4:

Country Action Program

- Utilizing "Data Power"
- Setting Institutional Priorities
- Concrete & Specific Implementation of Reforms
- Pilot Activities
- Political Will and Government Role
- Civil Society/NGOs
- Parliament
- Role of International Community/ OECD/Donors
- Expertise Inputs

Source: Kaufmann, Pradhan and Ryterman (1998)

Exhibit 7.4

EMPRICS PERMITS "GRADUATION"

FROM	→	TO
1. Rhetoric	→	Facts To Mobilize
2. "Ethics" Focus	→	Technocratic Program
3. Moralizing	→	Developmental
4. Individualized	→	Systemic Approach
5. Symptom	→	Address Fundamentals
6. Enforcement	→	Prevention and Incentives
7. Institution Building	→	Institutional Revamp
8. Generality	→	Agency- Specific
9. "Christmas-Tree" Lists	→	Prioritized Actions
10. Legal "Projects"	→	"Beyond Rule of Law"
11. National	→	With Municipalities

Towards In-depth Corruption Diagnostics: A Summary

The main points stressed in this section can be summarized as follows. We require a *focused but multi-pronged* approach for the measurement and diagnostics of corruption. Corruption assessments require measurement from various complementary angles, yet require a focus on a limited tool kit in each case in order to carry out the assessment within a reasonable budgetary and time framework. The mix of measurement instruments will vary from setting to setting, but will typically include some existing survey and hard data as well as a focused Greenfield interview instrument.

We have to *measure correlates* and potential *determinants* of corruption, moving beyond merely measuring corruption indicators. Evaluation and diagnosis of key potential determinants of corruption is of fundamental importance. In addition, we need to identify variables that interact with corruption for an action-oriented design of programs.

Areas of particular focus and analytical framework driving corruption diagnostic will *vary from country to country*. Key potential areas and approaches need to be identified through overall country knowledge. Public economics, institutional change, civil sector performance and pay, monopolized "target" sectors (such as energy in many countries), and unsupervised financial sectors provide alternative vantage points of analysis. Links between public sector institutional performance (governance) and corruption are typically emphasized. The importance of assessing the problem from the standpoints of public economics (budgetary, tax and regulatory regimes), as well as from a financial sector perspective (as suggested by the problems faced by East Asia and transition economies), however, needs to be emphasized much more.

Technocratic rigor in diagnostic and interpretation – from measurement to diagnostic, and from diagnostic to action programs – is critical. Special care is needed in *interpreting the multiple-survey and "hard" data* for the diagnostic assessment, and then in translating in-depth diagnostics into specific action program recommendations. Proximate causes (and symptoms) of corruption need to be distinguished from *fundamental causes* of corruption. Data analysis needs to have a simple analytical framework behind it. In performing the empirical analysis, it is useful to place the country data in an international comparative context, where corruption indicators are put alongside its possible determinants across many countries. This helps flag which potential determinants of corruption worldwide may apply in particular to the country under in-depth study, and aids in honing on the broad priorities for designing an anti-corruption program.

The power of activist data. Measurement is far more than a diagnostic or research tool; it is an activist tool helping correct deliberate information asymmetries (and secretiveness and obscurantism). It is key for raising awareness within civil society and aiding reformists in government.

Ultimately, the objective becomes to *integrate the various diagnostic instruments into one technocratic and unified framework of analysis and action program design.*

ANTI-CORRUPTION PROGRAMS: THE EVIDENCE

The data gathering exercise sketched above can provide insightful information as a crucial input to an overall diagnostic and anti-corruption action plan. The suggested approach to measurement is likely to identify forms of corruption, its correlates, and a number of proximate causes. Further, the in-depth survey diagnostics tools can provide substantial agency-specific information, which is essential for detailing the proposed institutional reform actions.

Yet we need to be conscious of the limits of the data as well as of the inductive empirical approach. While the data may tell us much about some of the direct, proximate causes of corruption, it may not in itself shed all the expected light on the more indirect, yet fundamental determinants of corruption. Political as well as economy-wide institutional and policy determinants, for instance, cannot be easily captured through field surveys. Analytical frameworks of analysis of corruption need to complement the survey and the other (more aggregate/macro) data gathering exercise. The leap from data analysis to program design needs careful thinking. Just because we find that very few of the many corrupt officials are being caught and prosecuted does not mean that instituting an anti-corruption watchdog body or passing another charter or decree will make a difference.

Nonetheless, there are ways of getting additional mileage from the data for action programs. Two examples will illustrate this point. First, we can compare the country performance rating on corruption and on its correlates with international data. Given empirical findings of what drives corruption worldwide, placing correlates of corruption within a country in an international context will provide "flags" on determinants to focus on. Second, gathering data on prices of generic goods in different localities in the country can provide a clear link to policy actions in public expenditures. "Inefficient" localities with very high unit costs would face cut backs in budgetary allocations as well as be subject to audits.

Finally, to place the issue of measurement in some perspective, let us note that we need to guard against the danger of *over-measuring and under-performing*. In some countries the dire need at this stage is less for an in-depth time consuming diagnostic, much more for real urgent actions.

Enough data exists for these countries to know basically what needs to be done during the first phase of an anti-corruption program. The rest of the information can be gathered gradually and pragmatically while program implementation starts.

TRANSLATING RESEARCH INTO ACTION:
SELECTED OPERATIONAL CHALLENGES

A. Identification of key underlying fundamentals. The main variables that need *emphasis* need to be identified. In addition, there is a need to recognize their interrelationships and sequencing. These variables may be legal, institutional, economic, tax-related, or pertaining to regulations. Similarly, we need to consider not only the conventional formal rules and institutions, but also the informal rules for strengthening institutions. Choices will also have to be made regarding the emphasis to be placed on government, legal and judicial institutions, civil society, or media.

B. Emphasis in policy formulation. Should the attention be focused on *freestanding or enclaving* anti-corruption interventions or should the emphasis be on *mainstreaming within broad reform programs?* Are there trigger or pressure points from pilots or islands of integrity that create demonstration effects and virtuous cycle dynamics? Should the "graduation" from enclaving (or pilots) to mainstreaming (or broader program) take place at a very early stage, given complementarities and necessary preconditions in some of the broader fundamentals?

If the choice is made in favor of mainstreaming, what are the relative roles of conventional versus "unconventional" mainstreaming instruments? Among the unconventional instruments, one may include, for instance, the issue of the appropriate policy design on taxation and civil service wages. These often deviate from conventional policy advise.

C. What role *institutional innovations* are likely to play and what are their *complementarities* with economic reforms? What is likely to be the role of World Bank and other lending/non-lending international institutions?

D. How much importance is to be given to *enforcement and control* mechanisms versus *incentives* and systemic reforms in addressing corruption?

E. Are the overall anti-corruption measures likely to *complement or conflict* with macroeconomic objectives? If *a priori* there are any tradeoffs, what measures can be taken to ameliorate them?

F. *Rebuilding country reputation on corruption.* Does reputational history-dependency justify special interventions to improve reputation when reform fundamentals are being addressed?

G. *Improving information flows* and *knowledge.* How best to create millions of "auditors" in the society who will create an environment for monitoring corruption activities?

H. *Methodological* innovations for action implementation. These actions may include, for example, corruption-mitigating approaches to public procurement and concessions in infrastructure projects, where research-based innovations are taking place with potentially large practical payoffs.

I. Emerging research findings will most likely strongly point to the *benefits of collective action.*[19] The suitability of collective action will go beyond non-bribery pledges through securing the collaboration of the international investment and trade community. The international investment community is likely to find in their interest to organize itself and pre-commit to not resort to bribes, if the appropriate "compact" is in place with the country leadership's commitments to reform.[20]

J. *Disseminating* operational research and its implications. There is a special need for a more activist strategy for dissemination of research findings and data on corruption.

CONCLUDING REMARKS

We end by being brief, in contrast with the rest of the chapter, espousing how, at this juncture, it is critical to deepen our understanding of the empirical dimension of corruption challenge. Within such empirics, furthering the study of the negative *consequences* of corruption may exhibit diminishing returns in the near future, since a consensus and general awareness is now emerging as to the ill-effects of corruption.

The same is not the case, however, with respect to the empirical understanding of the *causes* of corruption, where additional research is indeed warranted. Further, complementing the general study of the causes of corruption (through worldwide empirical analysis) with in-depth country case studies is likely to have high payoffs. We need to understand better why there is such paucity of successful public sector reforms around the world, for instance (and why a focus on civil service pay may not have paid off either). Agency-specific micro-studies within countries (customs, tax administration, and courts) can provide significant added insights, as would specific case studies for particular types of corruption.[21]

The ongoing buildup of more extensive data bases on governance and corruption indicators are permitting a rise in corruption-related research, one that is already challenging prevailing myths from the recent "prose" or "pure theory" era. Much further work in data gathering, and analysis is needed, however, in the next stage. In this stage, the evolution between general empirical research, in-depth country diagnostics through rigorous surveys, and the design of operationally relevant action programs is proving to be both feasible and valuable: this process is already resulting in added technocratic credibility to corruption assessments, awareness raising and the recommended options. And the emerging policy and institutional recommendations from this framework go further than the conventional recommendations that prevailed prior to approaching anti-corruption from a more rigorous empirical standpoint.

ACKNOWLEDGEMENTS

I am indebted to numerous collaborators at the World Bank and Harvard University (where this work was initiated). Views, errors and omissions are the author's, and do not necessarily reflect the institution's.

NOTES

[1]   See Bardhan 1997 for a survey. Also see Elliot 1997.

[2]   As a result, some important research topics are omitted. Some issues considered important by other contributors to this book may not be emphasized here. This in no way signals a lesser priority of those issues since this essay does not claim to be all-encompassing. There are likely to be disagreements on commission as well, since I will argue that the next phase of research ought to place significant emphasis on rigorous empirical research. This should be done not only for furthering the basic understanding of issues heretofore subject to either long prose or mere theoretical formulations, but for its potential contribution to identifying practical and implementable remedies to corruption.

3   One exception may be Klitgaard 1988.

4   The broad consensus of the first stage has not been fundamentally challenged in spite of
     the fact that second-generation issues have emerged in both fields - such as the mild and
     sporadic interventionist implications of "strategic" trade policy, fixed versus floating
     exchange rate regimes, and the precise degree of fiscal "austerity" and interest rate levels
     desired (particularly controversial in the case of the recent East Asia crisis). Some of
     these debates are discussed in The World Bank (1987) and The World Bank (1991).

5   Examples would include contributions by B. Balassa, A. Kruger, J. Bhagwati, M.
     Corden, for example, on the opening of trade regimes, M. Bruno and S. Fischer on
     macro-fundamentalism, J. Sachs and R. Dornbush on both the above issues as well as on
     the exchange rate regime linkages.

6   Insufficient attention to this issue often results in an absence of rigour in important
     empirical initiatives. For instance, even the widely cited cross-country Transparency
     International's Corruption Perception Index has been ambiguous as to whether it captures
     a proxy for perceptions about corruption generally in a country, or whether it is meant to
     concentrate more on certain forms of corruption in particular, such as bribery – as
     reported by particular units of observation, such as firms. There is an ongoing attempt to
     rectify such deficiency; which *inter alia* would have methodological implications as to
     how best to re-calculate and interpret such index.

7   See, for example, Lui 1985.

8   This taxonomy was developed with colleagues working on transition economies, where
     this framework was first applied. For details, see Kaufmann, Bardhan and Ryterman
     1998.

9   See, for example, arguments by Leff (1964) and Huntington (1964) more than twenty
     years ago, and Lui (1985) and others, also in the academe, more recently. Such view were
     often espoused by experts for the case of East Asia until the recent crisis.

10   The underlying "true" relationship between corruption and a host of economic
     development variables may well be very robust, but such relationship is likely to be
     difficult to measure and verify.

11   Corruption affects public finances by reducing the level of tax revenues, among other
     ways.

12   Furthermore, it is important to note that even if predictability of corruption were to
     matter empirically, a key question would be to consider the dynamic path of corruption
     within a country, and thus to ponder whether such predictability is sustainable. Highly
     corrupt environments may sustain predictable and well organized (as per next point)
     corruption for some length of time, but not forever, as it became painfully clear in East
     Asia recently. Thus, this area of predictability of corruption is far from settled

empirically, and further research would be beneficial and likely to yield some operational insights.

[13] While admittedly preliminary at this stage, it may be speculated that an empirical investigation into this issue may suggest that both matter significantly, and that in most settings both types of corruption are highly correlated with each other.

[14] Shleifer and Vishny 1998. Earlier works include Grossman and Hart 1984, and Jain 1987, 1988, and 1993. Also see Johnston 1997.

[15] Further details on the exhibits included in this appendix can be found in Kaufman, Pradhan, and Ryterman 1998. These exhibits have been prepared from the data gathered in Albania by a joint survey conducted by ACER and The World Bank and in Georgia by GORBI and The World Bank.

[16] See Chapter 5 in this volume.

[17] The precise rating given to each country ought to be interpreted instead as falling within a very broad range of possible values; further some country rankings in particular have been challenged.

[18] If the objective is to test with statistical rigor the relationship between corruption and other variables, often the preferred route ought to be utilizing a variety of independent single source measurements of corruption -- and exploring whether the hypothesis is borne out empirically in most or all different specifications (utilizing the different corruption variable).

[19] See Ruzindana 1997 for importance of this issue.

[20] See Rose-Ackerman 1997 and Rose-Ackerman and Stone 1996 for some issues concerning business involvement in bribery.

[21] As do, for instance, garbage collection and organized crime links to corruption in US cities at the turn of the century; or studying anthropologically the whole corrupt chain in a corrupt port.

REFERENCES

Ades, A. and R. Di Tella. (1997). "National Champions and Corruption: Some Unpleasant Interventionist Arithmetic." *The Economic Journal* 107: 1023-1042.

Bardhan, Pranab. (1997). "Corruption and Development: A Review of Issues." *Journal Of Economic Literature*, 35: 1320-1346.

Elliot, Kimberly Ann, (Ed.) (1997). *Corruption and the Global Economy*. Washington DC: Institute for International Economics.

Gray, Cheryl W., and Daniel Kaufmann. (1998). "Corruption and Development," *Finance and Development*, 35 (1): 7-10.

Grossman, Sanford J., and Oliver Hart. (1984). "The Costs and Benefits of Ownership: A Theory of Vertical and Lateral Integration." *Journal of Political Economy*. 94 (4): 691-719.

Huntington, Samuel P. (1964). "Modernization and Corruption," Arnold J. Heidenheimer, (ed.) *Political Corruption: Readings In Comparative Analysis*, New York: Holt Reinehart, 492-500.

Jain, Arvind K. (1987). "Agency Problem and the International Debt Crisis." Proceedings of the Fourth Symposium on Money, Banking, and Insurance (Geld, Banken und Versicherungen), Karlsruhe, West Germany, Band I: 367-91.

_____. (1988). "An Agency Theoretic Explanation of Capital Flight," *Economics Letters*, Vol. 28, no. 1, 1988, 41-5.

_____. (1993). "Dictatorships, Democracies, and Debt Crisis." In S. P. Riley, (ed.), *The Politics of Global Debt*, New York: St. Martin's Press.

Johnston, Michael. (1997). "Public Officials, Private Interests, and Sustainable Democracy: When Politics and Corruption Meet," in Kimberly Ann Elliot (ed.), *Corruption and the Global Economy*, Washington D.C.: Institute for International Economics, 61-82.

Johnson, Simon, Daniel Kaufmann, and Pablo Zoido-Lobaton. (1998). "Regulatory Discretion and the Unofficial Economy," *American Economic Review*, 88: 387-392.

Johnson, Simon, Daniel Kaufmann, and Andrei Shleifer. (1997). "The Unofficial Economy in Transition," Brookings Papers on Economic Activity, (2): 159-239.

Kaufmann, Daniel, and Jeffrey Sachs. (1998). "Determinants of Corruption," Harvard University: Unpublished manuscript.

Kaufmann, Daniel, Sanjay Pradhan, and Randi Ryterman. (1998). "New Frontiers in Anti-Corruption Empirial Diagnostics: From In-Depth Survey Analysis to Action Programs in Transition Economies." World Bank Economic Development Institute: Unpublished working paper.

Kaufmann, Daniel, and Shan-Jin Wei. (1998). "Does 'Grease Money' Speed up the Wheels of Commerce?" Paper presented at the American Economic Association Meeting, Chicago.

Kaufmann, Daniel, and Pablo Zoido-Lobaton. (1998). "Unpredictability and Corruption." World Bank Economic Development Institute: Unpublished working paper.

Klitgaard, Robert. (1988). *Controlling Corruption*, Berkeley: University of California Press.

Leff, Nathaniel H. (1964). "Economic development through bureaucratic corruption," in Arnold J. Heidenheimer, (ed.) *Political Corruption: Readings In Comparative Analysis*, New York: Holt Reinehart, 8-14.

Lui, Francis. (1986). "An Equilibrium Queuing Model of Bribery," *Journal of Political Economy*, 93: 760-781.

Newman, Peter, (Ed.) (1998). *New Palgrave Dictionary of Economics and Law*, UK: MacMillan Stockton Press.

Mauro, Paolo. (1997). "The Effects of Corruption on Growth, Investment, and Government Expenditure: A Cross–Country Analysis," in Kimberly Ann Elliot (ed.), *Corruption and the Global Economy*, Washington D.C.: Institute for International Economics, 83–107.

Rose-Ackerman, Susan. (1997). "The Political Economy of Corruption," in Kimberly Ann Elliot (ed.), *Corruption and the Global Economy*, Washington D.C.: Institute for International Economics, 31-60.

Rose-Ackerman, Susan, and Andrew Stone. (1996). "The Costs of Corruption for Private Business: Evidence from the World Bank Survey," World Bank: Manusacript.

Ruzindana, Augustine. (1997). "The Importance of Leadership in Fighting Corruption in Uganda," ," in Kimberly Ann Elliot (ed.), *Corruption and the Global Economy*, Washington D.C.: Institute for International Economics, 133-145.

Shleifer, Andrei, and Robert Vishny. (1994). "The politics of market socialism," *Journal of Economic Perspectives*, 8 (2): 165-176.

_____, (Eds.) 1998. *The Grabbing Hand: Government Pathologies and Their Cures*. Cambridge, Mass: Harvard University Press, (forthcoming).

Stapenhurst, Rick, and Sahr Kpundeh (Eds.) (1998, forthcoming). *Curbing Inflation*. Washington D.C.: Economic Development Institute, The World Bank.

Tanzi, Vito, and Hamid Davoodi. (1997). "Corruption, Public Investment, and Growth." IMF Working Paper WP/97/139.

The World Bank. (1987). *World Development Report*. New York: Oxford University Press.

The World Bank. (1991). *World Development Report: The Challenge of Development*. New York: Oxford University Press.

The World Bank. (1997).*World Development Report: The State in the Changing World*. New York: Oxford University Press.

Tornell, Aaron, and Philip Lane. (1998). "Voracity and Growth." *The American Economic Review*, (forthcoming).

Wei, S. J. (1997). "How Taxing is Corruption on International Investors." Washington D.C.: NBER Working Paper 6030.

Appendix 7.1

IN-DEPTH COUNTRY CORRUPTION DIAGNOSTICS: THE FOUR-PRONGED APPROACH

Typology of Corruption and Survey Instruments

	1.	2a.	2b.	2c.	3.	4.
Type of Corruption	Enterprise Survey	Survey of Government Officials	Judicial Officials' Component of Survey	Parlia-mentary Component of Survey	Household/ Citizen Survey	Other Instruments— "Hard Data", etc.
I. BRIBES						
A. ECONOMIC-/REGULATORY						
Speed Payments (Reduce delays)	x	x	x	x	x	Measuring Actual Delays
Better Service Delivery		x			x	Measuring service quality
Evasion of Economic Regulations	x	x	x	x		Balance of Payments and Customs Data Analysis
Tax Evasion/- Exemptions	x	x			x	Scheduled vs. actual VAT collections

Appendix 7.1 (page 2)

IN-DEPTH COUNTRY CORRUPTION DIAGNOSTICS: THE FOUR-PRONGED APPROACH

Evasion of environmental regulations	x	x			
Evasion of security regulations (Nuclear, etc)					Reported incidents
Preferential treatment in procurement and contracts	x	x	X		Price comparison of publicly procured goods (PPC Initiative)
"Purchase" of property rights ("Special" privatization, etc.)	x	x	X	x	
Purchase of monopoly rights	?	x	X		
By foreign investors	x	x			Foreigner investors' propensity to bribe
Reduced harassment (road/police/health/fire inspectors)	x			x	

Appendix 7.1 (page 3)

IN-DEPTH COUNTRY CORRUPTION DIAGNOSTICS: THE FOUR-PRONGED APPROACH

Government official "protection" (from official extortion, etc)	x	?				
Condoning drug trade/smuggling	?					U.S. Dept. of State
Condoning money laundering	?					U.S. Dept. of State
Jobs allocated in exchange for bribes (see also patronage)	x	x	x	X		"Purchase fee" for job categories
B. LEGAL						
Purchase of justice		x	x	X	x	Use/effectiveness of courts measured through jurimetric analysis
• Criminal rulings		x				
• Civil rulings		x				
• Commercial rulings	x	x				

Appendix 7.1 (page 4)

IN-DEPTH COUNTRY CORRUPTION DIAGNOSTICS: THE FOUR-PRONGED APPROACH

Manipulation of the legal process						Jurimetric analysis
• Statutes	?		x			
• Regulations	x	?		x		
C. EDUCATIONAL						
Purchase of educational credentials (degrees/grades)					x	Interviewing graduates, parents, ex-teachers
II. THEFT						
Misappropriation of public *Budgetary Funds*		x				Public expenditure review
Misappropriation of *Public Assets*		x				
Misappropriation of (Public) *Foreign Exchange and Donor Aid*		x				Balance of payments analysis

Appendix 7.1 (page 5)

IN-DEPTH COUNTRY CORRUPTION DIAGNOSTICS: THE FOUR-PRONGED APPROACH

III. PATRONAGE					
Political allocation of labor/nepotism		X		X	Overemployment in Public Sector. Civil Service rotation when political regime changes
Senior official appointments (resulting from illegal payoffs)		X		X	Measuring payoffs to "acquire" job/position
Hiring of consultants (foreign and domestic) in exchange for bribes		X			Interview with donor agencies
IV. INFLUENCE PEDDLING					
Illegal contributions to political parties (for favoritism in contracts/policy regime)	X	X	?		Lexis/Nexus search
Illegal contributions to politicians' campaigns (for favoritism in contracts/policy regime)	X			?	Lexis/Nexus search

Appendix 7.2

APPLICATION OF CORRUPTION DIAGNOSTICS

ALBANIA: PUBLIC OFFICIAL'S PERCEPTION OF WHO PAYS TO GET JOBS

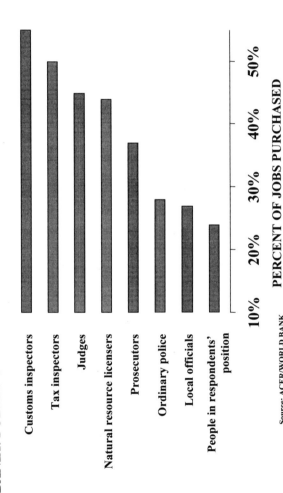

Source: ACER/WORLD BANK
Public Officials Survey, 1998.

Appendix 7.2 (page 2)

APPLICATION OF CORRUPTION DIAGNOSTICS

ALBANIA: PUBLIC OFFICIAL'S VIEWS ON DISHONESTY IN INSTITUTIONS

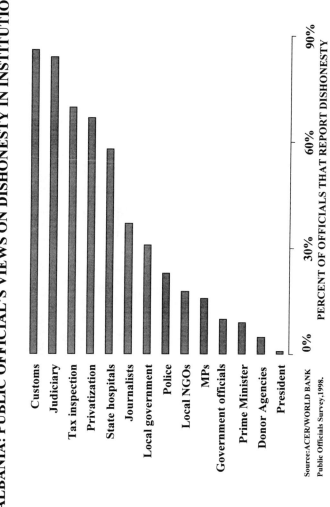

Source:ACER/WORLD BANK
Public Officials Survey,1998.

Appendix 7.2 (page 3)

APPLICATION OF CORRUPTION DIAGNOSTICS

ALBANIA: COMMON FORMS OF CORRUPTION IN GOVERNMENT

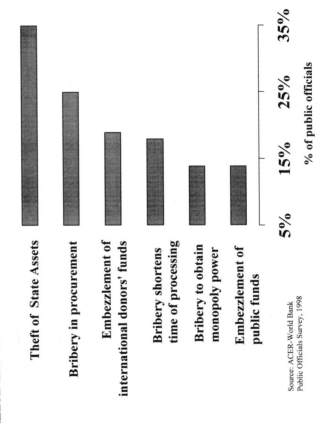

Source: ACER-World Bank
Public Officials Survey, 1998

Appendix 7.2 (page 4)

APPLICATION OF CORRUPTION DIAGNOSTICS

GEORGIA: BRIBE FREQUENCY TO PUBLIC AGENCIES

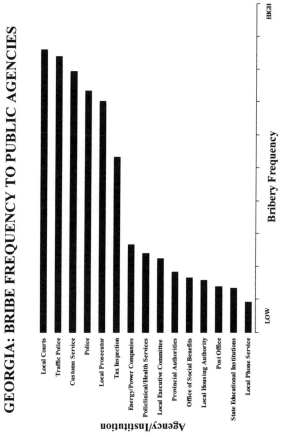

Source of Data: Gorbi/World Bank Enterprise Survey in 1998; See Kaufmann, Pradhan and Ryterman (1998)

Appendix 7.3

A "BRIBE" FEE LIST

Unofficial" Payments by Enterprises for Official Permits' Licenses and Services:
1996 Survey of Ukraine and Russia

TYPE OF LICENSE OR FAVOR	Average "unofficial" fee for the favor*	
	Ukraine	**Russia**
Enterprise registration	$ 176	$ 288
Each visit by fire/health inspector	$ 42	$ 67
Tax inspector (each regular visit)	$ 87	$ 250
Each phone line installation	$ 894	$ 1071
Lease of state-owned space (sq. meter/month)	$ 7	$ 26
Each export license/registration	$ 123	$ 643
Each import license/registration	$ 278	$ 133
Each border crossing (lump sum)	$ 211	(NA)
Each border crossing (percent of value)	3%	50%
Domestic currency loan from bank (Preferential terms)	4%	8%
Foreign currency loan from bank (Preferential terms)	4%	23%

* Average among those that admit making unofficial payments. Preliminary data based on March 1996 survey of 150 state/private enterprises in 5 large Ukrainian cities, and of 50 enterprises in three large Russian cities. Caution should be exercised in interpretation of the data, which are not representative of the whole country (particularly in Russia, where the sample is small).

CONTRIBUTING AUTHORS

ARVIND K. JAIN

Arvind K. Jain has been a faculty member at Concordia University in Montreal since 1990. He earned his Ph. D. from The University of Michigan, Ann Arbor. Before joining Concordia, he had taught at Indiana University, McGill University, The University of Michigan and the University of Dar es Salaam. He has held short-term or visiting appointments at University of Otago, New Zealand, Helsinki School of Economics, Finland, International University of Japan, and Tianjin University, China. Besides teaching, he has worked in industry or in public sector in India, the United States, Tanzania and Mexico. His current research focuses on impact of corruption on economic development, management of exchange risk, and capital markets. His past research papers dealing with agency theory and the debt crisis, capital flight, international lending decisions of banks, oligopolistic behavior in banking, foreign debt and foreign trade of developing countries, impact of culture on saving behavior, and commodity futures markets have appeared in *Journal of International Business Studies*, *Journal of Money, Credit and Banking*, *Economics Letters*, *Journal of Economic Psychology*, and other academic journals. He has written two book: *Commodity Futures Markets and the Law of One Price* (1981) and, *International Financial Markets and Institutions* (1994). He is on the editorial board of two journals, including the *Journal of International Business Studies*.

DANIEL KAUFMANN

Daniel Kaufmann, Lead Economist in the Development Economics Group of the World Bank, received his Masters and Ph. D. degrees in Economics at Harvard University, after obtaining degrees from the Hebrew University in Jerusalem. He has published in economic and public policy journals on issues of economic development, privatization, corruption, the unofficial economy and the informal sector, investment productivity, industrial and trade restructuring, and labor economics. Recently, he has concentrated on theoretical and empirical aspects of world-wide corruption, pioneering new methodologies to assess and diagnose corruption and regulatory and institutional constraints. He has also published and advised governments on action-oriented programs to implement institutional and regulatory reforms and address corruption. His country-specific advice and writings on corruption have recently covered, among others, many countries in Transition (such as Ukraine, Russia, Bulgaria and Albania) as well as countries in Latin America and Africa. With the World Bank he has worked in Transition Economies, Latin America, Africa and Asia. In the early-to-mid nineties he served as the Chief of Mission of the Bank in Ukraine. During 1996-1997 Dr. Kaufmann was at Harvard University, where in addition to teaching and research, he provided policy advise to emerging economies. The in-depth empirical assessment of the causes and consequences of corruption was an important area of concentration of his research and seminars at Harvard.

JOHANN GRAF LAMBSDORFF

Since 1992 Johann Graf Lambsdorff has been member of the economics faculty at Göttingen University, Germany. He earned his Ph. D. there in 1994, after obtaining degrees in mathematics, sociology and economics in Frankfurt am Main and Göttingen. In cooperation with Transparency International he has published the annual Corruption Perception Index since 1995, one of the most influential indices to appear in recent years which has drawn world attention and serves as a research tool to measure the impact of corruption on investment, growth, inequality, trade, etc. His current research focuses on corruption at the intersection of institutional economics, political economy, international trade and empirical research. His past research papers have dealt with the economics of corruption, theories of oligopolistic behavior, institutional economics, and the economics of raw materials. He is the author of two books dealing with open macroeconomics and economic teaching and his contributions have been published in the *Jahrbuch fuer Wirtschaftswissenschaften (Review of Economics)*, and in the *European Journal of Development Research*.

R. T. NAYLOR

R.T. Naylor is professor of economics at McGill Universityin Montreal. He has published several works on business history. During the last decade his major research interests have been smuggling, money-laundering, and enterprise crime. His best-known book, *Hot Money and the Politics of Debt*, has been translated into French, Spanish, Portugese, Italian, and Turkish. Much of his work has appeared in the journal *Crime, Law and Social Change* of which he is currently a senior editor. In addition to his McGill duties, he is a senior fellow of the Peach and Conflict Studies Program at the University of Toronto and a research associate of the Nathanson Centre for the Study of Crime and Corruption at York University in Toronto.

VITO TANZI

Vito Tanzi received his Ph.D. in economics from Harvard University. Before joining the International Monetary Fund in 1974, where he is Director of the Fiscal Affairs Department, he was Professor and Chairman, Department of Economics, at the American University. He has also been on the faculty of the George Washington University and a consultant for the World Bank, the United Nations, the Organization of American States, and the Stanford Research Institute. He has published many books including: *The Individual Income Tax and Economic Growth* (Johns Hopkins University Press, 1969); *Inflation and the Personal Income Tax* (Cambridge University Press, 1980); *The Underground Economy in the United States and Abroad* (Lexington Press, 1982); *Taxation, Inflation and Interest Rates* (IMF, 1984); *Public Finance in Developing Countries* (Edward Elgar, 1991); and *Taxation in an Integrating World* (Brookings, 1995). He has edited several books, the most recent of which is *Income Distribution and High Quality Growth* (MIT Press, 1998). He has written a large number of articles in leading professional journals, such as the *American Economic Review, The Journal of Political Economy, The Review of Economics and Statistics, The Economic Journal, The Journal of Public Economics*, and many others. His major interests are public finance, monetary theory, and macroeconomics. In the period 1990-94, he was President of the International Institute of Public Finance.

INDEX